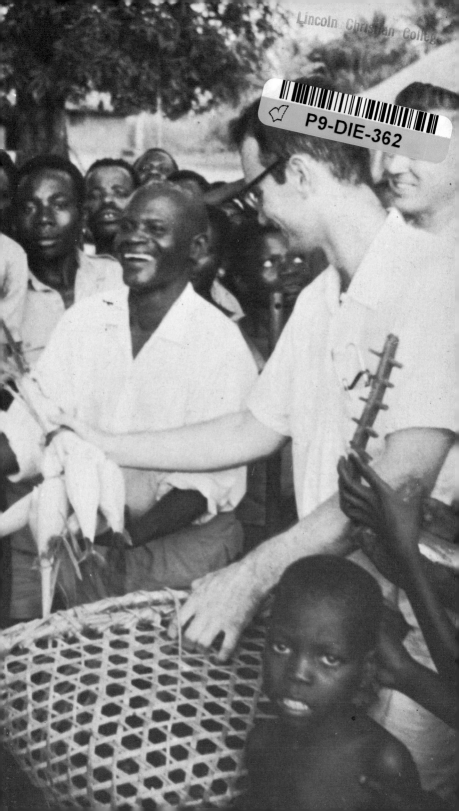

CONGO CRISIS

CONGO CRISIS

Charles and Muriel Davis Relive
an Era of Missions During Weeks
of Imprisonment in Stanleyville, Africa

JOSEPH T. BAYLY

ZONDERVAN PUBLISHING HOUSE

GRAND RAPIDS, MICHIGAN

To
THE CHURCH IN CONGO

Acknowledgments

I acknowledge my debt to the following:

The Africa Inland Mission and Unevangelized Fields Mission, for their complete cooperation.

Charles and Muriel Davis, Ione McMillan and her sons, for answering all my questions.

Barry Farber for the tape of his show (WOR, New York) on which Charles Davis was a guest. Martin G. Berck, New York *Herald Tribune*, for the transcript of his interview of Davis.

Assani Benedict and Daniel Makasi, Congolese pastors, for answering my questions and expressing their viewpoint. Marjie Mehlis for helping with an interview.

Peter and Mary Lou Stam, old friends, for their advice and comments about the Congo. The late Ralph Odman, and Majil — also old friends — for their special help in supplying missing parts of the story.

Friends who read the manuscript at various stages, and commented on various aspects: Virginia Krauss Hearn, Eugene W. Allen, and Robert B. Reekie (who also provided in-depth Africa knowledge).

Zondervan Publishing House, especially Floyd W. Thatcher and T. A. Bryant, for their encouragement and patience.

And, of course, Mary Lou — who is a fine critic — and our children, who prayed the book to completion.

I thank each one.

JOSEPH T. BAYLY

The Congo Martyrs

The following Protestant missionaries died during the general period of time covered by this book:

JOHN ARTON
ELIZABETH ARTON
  HEATHER ARTON
    Unevangelized Fields Mission   *England*

MARY BAKER
    Unevangelized Fields Mission   *United States*

CHESTER BURK
    Unevangelized Fields Mission   *Canada*

PAUL CARLSON
    Evangelical Covenant Church of America *United States*

IRENE FERREL
    Baptist Mid-Missions   *United States*

ROBINA GRAY
   Unevangelized Fields Mission   *Ireland*

MURIEL HARMON
   Worldwide Evangelization Crusade   *Canada*

BURLEIGH LAW
   Central Congo Methodist Mission   *United States*

LAUREL McCALLUM
   Unevangelized Fields Mission   *Australia*

WILLIAM McCHESNEY
   Worldwide Evangelization Crusade   *United States*

HECTOR McMILLAN
   Unevangelized Fields Mission   *Canada*

DENNIS PARRY
NORA PARRY
   ANDREW PARRY
   GRACE PARRY
   Unevangelized Fields Mission   *England*

PHYLLIS RINE
   Africa Christian Mission   *United States*

JAMES RODGER
   Worldwide Evangelization Crusade   *Scotland*

WILLIAM SCHOLTEN
   Unevangelized Fields Mission   *United States*

IAN SHARPE
AUDREY SHARPE
 JILLIAN SHARPE
 ALISON SHARPE
 ANDREW SHARPE
  Unevangelized Fields Mission   *England*

JEAN SWEET
  Unevangelized Fields Mission   *England*

CYRIL TAYLOR
  Worldwide Evangelization Crusade *New Zealand*

JOSEPH TUCKER
  Assemblies of God   *United States*

In addition, WINIFRED DAVIES (Worldwide Evangelization Crusade, *England*) is still listed as missing. Miss Davies has been reported seen in the Congo, and is presumed a prisoner of the Simba forces-in-hiding.

*   *   *

Names of Congolese Christian believers who died are known only to God, but their martyrdom is equally precious.

Foreword

Why another book about the Congo uprising of late 1964, in which Dr. Paul Carlson was killed?

In brief, because now the whole story can be told.

As I've pieced together the facts that have come out of Stanleyville in recent months, a small idea has grown and possessed my mind. The idea: this story is so significant that every person related to the church should hear it. Somehow the church in America, in Canada and Great Britain must be exposed to the greatness of the church in Congo.

Let me tell you what I mean.

Soon after his return from Stanleyville, Charles Davis was interviewed on the Barry Farber show (WOR, New York). Here's an excerpt from Farber's introduction: "Our guest today arrived in the studio with a horror-hardened reporter for the New York *Daily News*. This reporter told me, off to one side, in an admiring whisper — which in itself is rare for a big-city newspaperman — 'It's refreshing to meet someone like Reverend Davis who has a mission in life instead of a gimmick.' "

Not all missionaries have a mission; Charles Davis and the others in Congo did — like that "missionaries' missionary," Hector McMillan. Father of six sons, McMillan was killed only hours before a rescue party arrived. Yet "That family," says Davis, "was more ready for the death of their father than any other family I've ever known."

And the magnificent women: Mary Baker, Margaret Hayes, the brave ones at Kilometer 8. Only in recent months have their stories become known and accessible to a writer. Stories of hiding out in the tropical forest . . . of being forced to watch the mutilation and murder of beloved priests . . . of surrender to certain death in order to save a whole village from annihilation.

But national Christians do not always share the mission; the heroic Congolese did. Thirty white missionaries died at the hands of the Rebels, while ten thousand Congolese Christians were martyred. This is their story, the story of Jacques, whose ear was cut off. "Now will you join us?" the Simbas asked. "No," he replied, "I'm a Christian." Then they held his feet in the fire. "I'll never join you," he said. "I follow Christ."

This is also the story of Yonama Agondia, the male nurse who took charge of a hospital after the missionaries were forced to evacuate. He led 195 patients past Rebel gunfire and days of trekking through the tropical forest until they reached safety in Uganda. Not one died on the way. (I was especially touched by the tenderness of Christians, through whose tribe he passed in the end. Yonama was dead-tired, so they gave him a bicycle. But he didn't have enough strength to pedal, so they surrounded him and pushed him up the mountain to a point where he could coast down the other side to the

I haven't been able to record the heroism of every Congolese Christian and missionary who passed through the floodtide. But Hector McMillan, Mary Baker, Bo Martin and his twin brother Assani are symbols of the common Christian courage.

A few years ago, I wrote another book, a book that made me laugh. This book made me cry. But it's made me shout, too. Here are people with "a mission in life instead of a gimmick." Nothing is more desperately needed in our gimmick-oriented culture. Gimmicks like money and things and sex and status and security.

But I've tried to do more than just tell what happened. This book attempts to answer the question, "Why?" How do we explain the tragedy of recent Congo history? Why is the Congo church so strong?

And what are the lessons for other times, other lands?

There are some judgments about missionary work, too — past and future. Some may ask, quite properly, "Who is he to give his opinions?" I answer that I am not a foreign missionary. I am only a writer, but one who has been forced to think about what he hears and reads, even while he writes.

But God's work — to use Maitland's description of history — is, "a seamless web." This gives me hope that what I write out of involvement in the mission in America may be relevant to the mission overseas.

And I believe that I have a heart for foreign missions and the career people in God's foreign service.

This Congo story is beyond my telling, but I have done my best.

JOSEPH T. BAYLY

Bartlett, Illinois

Contents

CONGO CRISIS

1/Black Saturday

THE HOTEL WAS air-conditioned. That much could be said for it.

But all the guests — twice as many as would normally be accommodated on its two floors — were prisoners. Belgians and Americans, with a few other nationalities thrown in, it seemed almost by accident. Doctors, newsmen, plantation owners and directors, missionaries: all white. And all forbidden to leave their rooms.

Armed guards prowled the halls.

Some wives were in the hotel. But most were scattered about the countryside in little groups of brave, fearful women. The fortunate ones had been evacuated to Leopoldville. All of them were afraid of what a few days would bring, especially for their husbands in the Hotel des Chutes.

This was Stanleyville in November, 1964. Four years four months after Congo's independence day, that historic June 30 when the first Prime Minister, Patrice Lumumba, taunted King Baudouin of Belgium: "From today we Congolese are no longer your monkeys."

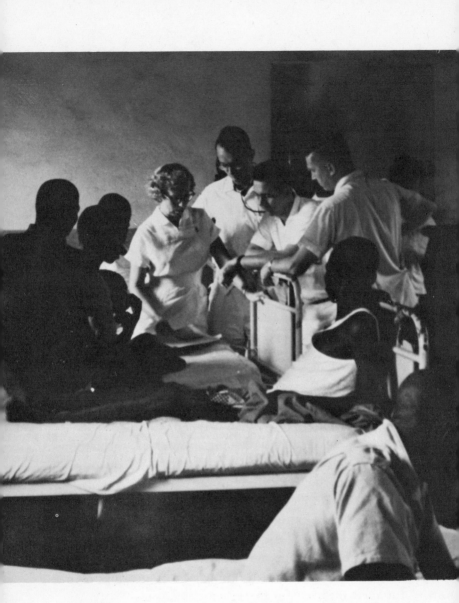

Dr. Paul Carlson and medical associates make ward rounds at Wasolo mission hospital the summer before Rebel uprising in which he was killed. *(Smith Kline & French Laboratories)*

Now the tables were turned, and Belgians — together with other whites — were the monkeys. Or so it must have seemed to the Congolese Rebels, their captors and keepers of the cage. "Simbas," they called themselves: Lions. Lions guarding monkeys in an air-conditioned cage, like the one at Copenhagen's Zoologisk Have, or Chicago's Brookfield Zoo.

"When did the Simbas first pick you up, Davis?" Dr. Marescotti, an Italian physician, asked the question.

"It was a Saturday afternoon in August. We were trying to get some rest after dinner when this officer with two Simbas came to the station. He said he was looking for four American citizens. According to him, all the Americans were to be evacuated. He said the American consular staff were waiting for us in Stanleyville."

"Wasn't the 'Hate America' campaign going on then? As I recall, the radio was full of it. They said all Americans were to be gathered together and killed. I don't understand why you believed that Simba major." The Italian doctor stopped talking and moved from the bed where he'd been sitting to stand by a window overlooking Stanleyville's business section. Simbas lounged in the road below.

"We hadn't been listening to the radio," Charles Davis replied, "so we didn't know. Besides, up to this time we'd been told that this was strictly a Congolese problem — brothers having a political dispute. White people weren't involved, they said."

"Who's 'they'?" Dr. Marescotti interrupted.

"Simbas who visited our mission station, demanding guns."

"But you didn't have any, did you?"

"No, but then they demanded gasoline, or something else. Later they demanded the automobile."

"That business of demanding rather than taking is a clever gambit, isn't it? What's the difference?" a portly Belgian planter asked.

"As far as we're concerned, none at all. But it makes a big difference to them. Simbas can't steal. Otherwise they're no longer protected by the witch doctor's *dawa*. If they steal, their immunity to bullets and other dangers no longer works. So they put a gun on the table or poke a rifle barrel in your stomach and say, 'I'd like that food — or radio — or pair of scissors.' You hand it over — or else. Afterward they say, 'Thank you, Bwana, for having given me this.' But we didn't give it — they took it.

"That other taboo of theirs, against any contact with the white man, is interesting, too. They think they'll lose the witch doctor's protection if they even touch a white man. So everything has to be placed on the ground, or handed over by being dropped from hand to hand." The planter gestured with his hands.

"They've got that other one, too, against attacking women," Dr. Marescotti added.

"But they do." The Belgian's voice was hard.

"Sure they do. They go to a village and say, 'We want so many chickens, so many eggs, so many stalks of bananas, so many women.' I don't know how they rationalize that with the *dawa*, but they do."

"Did they ever bother white missionary women, Davis?"

"Just once at our station. This drunk Simba came one night and demanded one of the missionaries. Al over there talked him out of it."

"What did you tell him, Larson?" An older man, lying on one of the beds, spoke for the first time.

Al Larson, senior missionary of the three imprisoned in the hotel room, answered briefly, then tried to change the subject.

"I just told him that we were Christians, and he couldn't have any of our women. — I wonder if that rumor about negotiations in Nairobi is true."

"The Simba was packing a .45 revolver, by the way, and had it aimed right at Al. So Al said, 'Now you just take your little gun and get out of here.' So he left after he'd routed everybody out of bed for an inspection."

"You were telling about what happened when they picked you up." Dr. Marescotti turned from the window toward Davis.

"Yes, it was a Saturday. I used to like Saturday, back home in Boston. Baked beans and hot dogs. But somehow or other I came to dislike the day during this Congo rebellion. So we were picked up in the middle of Saturday afternoon."

"You and your wife?"

"And our two children, Stephen, who's four, and Beth, who's not quite two."

"Weren't there any other missionaries at your station?" the portly Belgian asked.

"Yes, but they were left behind because they were Canadian and British. The Simbas were only looking for Americans this time."

"Because they blamed us for giving planes to Tshombe's government. And those planes are beginning to hurt," Del Carper — the third missionary in the room — explained.

"Let Davis get on with his story."

"Well, they took us into Stan in this blue Opel with an open top. There were two Simbas and an officer."

"Armed, of course."

"Yes, one Simba had a club, the other had a spear, and the officer had a revolver."

"Where'd they take you?"

"To Camp Kitele, here in Stan. There were hundreds of

CHARLES AND MURIEL DAVIS, first-term missionaries, with their children, Steve and Beth. The Davis family had only been in the Congo a few months when they were seized by Rebel forces and held as hostages.

troops there, and they all seemed to be arguing with each other. It was like a riot going on all around us when we pulled up. In the midst of all this confusion, there was a colonel arguing with two of his officers. Really dressing them down. So I was taken out of the car and brought to the colonel."

"Was it Opepe?"

"No, this was a different one. I don't know his name. Anyway, he ordered me back into the car and told the driver to get us out of there. So they turned the car around and started to leave when there were some shots and a Simba was shot down ahead of us. Then the soldiers began to manhandle another one to our right. They slammed him against the car, trying to knock him down. But he fought back. They finally got him down right behind the car, and then they began opening up their guns on him. They must have slammed 50 bullets into his body."

"Did your children see all this?"

"As plainly as we did. And a moment later there were about ten or twelve guns pointed at us through the car windows."

"What did you do?"

"Funny thing, when I checked with Muriel — that's my wife — later, I found we both did the same thing in those first couple of seconds. We both prayed that we'd all be shot."

"I don't understand. You prayed that you'd *all* be shot?"

"Yes, we didn't want to think of our children being left in all this madness if we were killed. And we were sure that our lives had come to an end. Remember, these rifles were still smoking from killing that man by the rear bumper. These were awfully excited Simbas — you know what they're like."

"We sure do. But they let you go. Why?"

"Only reason I can give is that the Lord protected us. He saw that no one got trigger-happy."

The Belgian's voice from the bed was soft. "I hope your Lord doesn't forget about us here."

"While you and your wife were praying that you'd all be shot, Davis, what did your children do?"

"Stephen cried. He kept saying over and over, 'Daddy, they shot that man.' I just put his head down on my lap while they were pushing the guns into the car. Muriel had Beth in her arms."

"But they let you go. They didn't harm you."

"No, they let us leave the camp. The officer who had brought us there drove us out to the airport. There we joined some of the American consulate people — Mike Hoyt and his staff. We were thrown into a women's water closet with them, and with some Congolese, about 17 of us in all. It was really a small space. The Americans had already spent the night there. They'd taken turns sleeping on the floor. It was pretty dirty — the toilet had backed up and the floor was all wet."

"Your wife and children, too?"

"Yes, they were there too, for about an hour. Then they came in and got Muriel and told her to go home — to take the children and go home. Ridiculous, but that's what they told her. So she left. I had to stand there and see the Simbas put her and the children back in the car and drive off with them. And she's pregnant."

The break up of families by force is an old story to the Congo.

British, Dutch, French, Danes and Swedes carried on the African slave trade during the 17th and 18th centuries. Americans joined the lucrative business in the 19th century.

Congolese parents were separated from their children, children from parents, husbands from wives, wives from husbands.

The death rate in transit was estimated at two out of three slaves. According to one authority, British ships supplied two million slaves — so the British alone must have left Africa with six million human beings.

This was what the Simbas were remembering as they separated the Davis family — and others — from one another.

2/Leopold's Ghost

PORTUGUESE TRADERS penetrated the Congo several decades before Columbus discovered America. Those early settlers introduced various plants from Brazil, cattle from their homeland, and the elements of Christianity.

During the Portuguese period of Congo history, every session of court was opened with these words: "Let not the money become black. Let not Christ the Redeemer be overturned. Speak but the truth; do not shame Christ. We, the chiefs, will not overturn the crucifix. We swear to deliver a just judgment."

In 1523, the grandson of King Nzinza Nkeuvu (convert to Christianity before the end of the previous century) became a bishop of the Catholic Church. This period of Congo's history was its Golden Age; prospects for education and progress seemed very bright.

But the enlightened era did not last.

A few years later the slave trade broke upon the Congo, ending Christian advance for the next three centuries. "Black ivory" became the Congo's most valuable commodity. Intertribal warfare ceased to be merely a competition for local dominance; it became the means of securing prisoners for sale to white traders in exchange for rum and trinkets. War parties often set fire to villages at night, capturing the villagers as they sought to escape the flames.

No one can estimate the suffering and injustice of those centuries, or the tides of bitterness and hatred that began to flow then . . . and still have not ebbed.

When the slave trade was finally halted in the nineteenth century, the white man had a certain image. To the Congolese, he was a bleached-out ghost who lived under the ocean. He came in ships that rose out of the water (the appearance of a ship that comes from over the horizon), and returned with cargoes of slaves. The image has been a hard one to overcome.

When the slave trade ended, a period of fresh exploration began. If the Congo could not supply human beings to make white fortunes, perhaps it could supply something else of value.

David Livingstone was one of the first to take something of value to the Congo: the Christian Gospel. As a medical missionary, he preceded Paul Carlson by 90 years. Actually, it was Livingstone's desire to find the watersheds that divide the great river basins of Central Africa that brought him to the Congo from Cape Town.

Henry M. Stanley's name became inseparably linked with that of Livingstone through his search for the missionary-explorer in 1871. The search—which was successful—resulted in his life-long interest in Africa, especially in the Congo.

Stanley failed to involve the British in this large African land area, but his exploration stirred the interest of Belgium's King Leopold II. As a private individual, Leopold founded the International Association of the Congo, which supported Stanley's later explorations. Leopold was also the major financial backer. This decision paid off in 1884, when the Congo Free State was established under Leopold's personal rule.

King Leopold remained aloof from the Congo and its problems, ruling the region through an administrator. This man appointed officials in the various areas, and gave them almost unlimited power. At the same time, the authority of tribal chiefs was downgraded—a pattern of government opposite to the British system. Congolese had no legal rights, and the European officials were free of restraint on their actions. It is not surprising that the record of Leopold II's Congo Free State was one of unsurpassed tyranny and cruelty in the modern world.

Leopold and the companies to which he granted concessions in the Congo had one interest: money. This money came from rubber and ivory, and depended upon the availability of plentiful free labor. This labor was exacted from the Congolese as a form of taxation. Actually, the system was slavery, and exceedingly brutal slavery. Armed guards were mounted on the workers, who were treated as prisoners. Their wives were sometimes taken as hostages when production quotas were not met, or as punishment for some infraction of rules. Brutal floggings were frequent, and the Congolese were sometimes maimed — their hands cut off — as an object lesson, to cause others to meet their production schedule.

Worldwide reaction to the absolute rule of Leopold II in the Congo was one of revulsion. The British particularly protested against the atrocities, although their reaction may have been increased by anger at their exclusion from participation in the profits from the Congo.

In America, Vachel Lindsay celebrated Leopold's death in a section of his poem, *The Congo*:

A roaring, epic, rag-time tune
From the mouth of the Congo
To the Mountains of the Moon.
Death is an Elephant,
Torch-eyed and horrible,
Foam-flanked and terrible.
Boom, steal the pygmies,
Boom, kill the Arabs,
Boom, kill the white men,
Hoo, Hoo, Hoo.
Listen to the yell of Leopold's ghost
Burning in Hell for his hand-maimed host.
Hear how the demons chuckle and yell
Cutting his hands off, down in Hell.

In 1910, after Leopold's death, the Belgians instituted a number of reforms in the Congo. This was a mere 50 years before independence, which came in 1960.

The Congolese advance toward independence during this half-century is perhaps more surprising than the barbarism and cruelty of the Rebels in recent months.

An increasingly enlightened Belgian government policy and the work of Christian missionaries made this advance possible.

From the time of Livingstone until 1960, when the Congo achieved independence, Christian missions were to a greater or lesser degree identified with the Belgian government's goals. Because Belgium was largely Roman Catholic, and because the Vatican defended Leopold II's government of the Congo, the Catholic Church had a favored position during Belgian rule. Priests had a civil status and were paid salaries by the colony. Education was under Church control, and subsidies were paid by the government.

Protestant missions did not share many Catholic advantages in the Congo, but received subsidies from the government for their schools after 1952.

Mission schools are responsible for the great advance in Congolese literacy, for when the modern missionary movement began in 1878, the Congo was totally illiterate. Hundreds of different languages spoken in the Congo region made the task vastly more difficult. These languages have been a great challenge to the missionary translator.

After 86 years of missionary work, the Congo at the time of the Rebel uprising had nearly three times as many Protestant missionaries, proportionate to the population, as the average for Africa (Congo: 1 to 6,000; Africa: 1 to 17,000).

But education and spiritual light were almost extinguished in Stanleyville that August night, as Muriel Davis and her two children rode away from the airport. The Simba soldiers at her side seemed the personification of cruelty and evil.

3/One Light in Stanleyville

STANLEYVILLE'S EVANGELICAL LIBRARY and bookstore (known as LECO, the initials of its name in French) was securely bolted for the night. One light shone from a second-floor window.

All sorts of rumors were abroad in the city that Saturday night, August 22, and the Jenkinsons were being more than usually careful. Forty-three years in the Congo had made them wise in times of danger.

In their apartment above the bookstore, Kinso and Ma Kinso (as they were known to the other missionaries, from the middle letters of their name) were reading. They did not have the radio on, and the only sounds came from insects buzzing around the light.

"Kinso!" The voice, a woman's, with an edge of desperation to it, came from the street below.

Immediately the man ran down the stairs and unlocked the door. As he threw it open, a young American woman with two children raced past him up the stairs without a word. She was carrying a baby girl, while a little boy held on to her skirt.

She stopped when she came into the lighted area and saw the grandmotherly woman.

"Oh, how thankful I am that you heard me!"

"Sit down, my dear, and then you can tell us who you are and what you're running from. But you're safe now. Here, let me take the baby."

"I'm Muriel Davis, and these are my two children, Stephen and Beth. They're holding my husband prisoner out at the airport. The Simbas* are, I mean. They picked us up this afternoon out at our station — Banjwadi — and they just let me and the children out of a car down on the street a few minutes ago."

"You can tell us about everything that's happened after we've taken care of the children. Would they like some cocoa? I'll make some for them, and then we can put them to bed. I don't doubt they need it — and so do you."

After Steve and Beth were in bed, Muriel told the Jenkinsons what had happened.

"The Lions picked us up this afternoon at Banjwadi. We're with the Africa Inland Mission, and Chuck was to teach at the school there. We've only been in the Congo a few months. When they came, this officer said they were going to evacuate all the Americans and we were supposed to go with them. So we did, although we didn't have any choice even if we hadn't believed him.

"They brought us into Stan all right, but instead of evacuating us, they took us to an army camp. There it was awful — I can't tell you how bad it was. A Lion was shot to death just outside the car, right where the children could see it, too. We tried to hush them up, because you know how angry the Lions

*The word Simba means lion in the Swahili language. This was what the Rebel soldiers called themselves. In this book, the words Simba and Rebel are used interchangeably, usually dependent on what the person being interviewed called them.

get when someone cries for one of their victims. But for some reason the officer at the camp didn't hold us there — he sent us away with the three Lions who'd brought us. And they drove us out of the camp, to the Stan airport.

"In the car, this Lion major who was holding a gun on us asked Chuck for his watch and his wedding band. So of course Chuck had to give them to him. As soon as I saw that, I took off my rings and stuck them in the front of my dress. I didn't want that major to have them, even if he shot me. Well, he didn't get them, although he did take my watch.

"When we got out of the car at the airport, this major kept shoving us with his revolver and telling us to move faster. We were going as fast as we could, but they kept saying, 'Hurry up! Hurry up!' They kept hitting me on the head because I wasn't going fast enough. Of course, I was carrying Beth. Chuck was up front with the suitcase, sort of pulling Steve along.

"Inside the airport building, they took us into this women's toilet — water all over the floor.

"We walked in, and there was the American consul and the members of his staff. They all said, 'Oh, no!' They couldn't believe that a woman and children would be in that place.

"I had this small bag I'd packed, with diapers and a few things for the baby, and the Lions took that away from me and kept it. It had all my personal stuff in it — wallet, glasses, things like that. But they took it and didn't return it.

"After about 40 minutes or so, they ordered us all outside and made us sit down. Then they stood up in front of us with their guns pointed at us. One of them was tossing shells on the floor so we'd be impressed with how well-equipped they were. All the while they were telling us how bad America was, and really yelling at us.

"Then all of a sudden, this man in charge looked at me and

said, 'Go home!' I really thought he was nuts. But I said, 'And my children, too.'

"He said, 'Yes, and your children, too.' But he wouldn't let me get the suitcase Chuck had carried in. Chuck wanted to give it to me, but he said no, that Chuck would stay right where he was.

"So I went out with just my two children, Steve and Beth. They put us in a car, and we got settled down. Then they came up and said, 'Get out.' I didn't know what they planned to do with us, but we got out. Then they made us get in another car.

"The Lion who was driving the car said, 'Where's your home?' I told him the Lions had brought us in from it that afternoon, and it was 64 kilometers away (40 miles), at Banjwadi.

"He didn't want to go that far. And he was getting angry because I didn't understand his Swahili and he couldn't understand my French. So I said, 'Well, could you take me to Kilometer 8?' You see, I didn't know anything at all about Stanleyville, but I did know there were missionaries at Kilometer 8.

"But he said, '*Which* Kilometer 8?' And I suddenly had a sinking feeling, because I had no idea at all what road the mission station was on."

"You must have been praying a lot right then."

"I sure was. I just kept asking the Lord to give me wisdom — help me know what to say and what to do. And I was feeling more and more desperate, because Steve was crying, and the one Lion kept telling him to shut up.

"So finally they stopped by the side of the road and called a Greek man over to the car. He was just passing by. They asked if he could speak English. (I guess they were beginning to feel really frustrated trying to talk to me in French.) He said yes, he spoke a little English. So they told him to tell me that they were going to take me to the military camp for the night. Then they'd take me to Kilometer 8 the next morning, they said."

"The thought of staying overnight in that army camp must have terrified you."

"I couldn't bear the thought of it. And I just kept praying hard, when the Lord laid on my mind this place — LECO. I asked the Greek man if he knew where it was. He didn't, but there was a Congolese man standing behind him, and he knew; it was just a block up the street from where we were. You can imagine how thrilled I was.

"The Lions let me out on the sidewalk. Of course, I'd never met you folks — I'd only heard about the bookstore and you. I didn't even know your full name — all I knew was Kinso. I didn't even know whether you lived in the building or not. You might have lived miles from here.

"But when the Lions drove off, I just walked around the building trying to decide how to get in. Suddenly I saw this light up here. I've never been so glad to see anyone in my whole life as I was to see you come to the door, Mr. Kinso. I guess I didn't even say anything — I just ran up the stairs."

"I think we'd better get to bed. It's almost Sunday already. But first, we'll have some prayer for your husband and the others who are having trouble tonight. You know you're welcome to stay here as long as necessary — until it's safe for you to leave, or your husband comes for you."

4/The Tragedy of Lumumba

THE SHADOW OF LUMUMBA overcast Stanleyville during those months late in 1964, even though he had been killed almost four years before.

Prisoners — Americans, Belgians, Congolese — would soon be led by Simbas to the Lumumba monument, almost daily, for execution. And other prisoners, fearfully awaiting the summons to a death march, would remember and discuss the man who played so prominent a part in opening the Pandora's box of Congo.

Patrice Lumumba grew up in Stanleyville, the son of nominally Christian parents. This man who would one day have a university in Moscow named for him received only a primary school education. But in this he was rather typical, for the Congo — unlike British colonies — had little secondary, and almost no higher education. As a result, the Congolese had no prepared cadre of educated leadership when independence came.

Not that Lumumba was uneducated. Even as a young man,

Patrice Lumumba (left
first Premier of Congo, u
der guard with another pri
oner, shortly before the
were killed. *(UPI)*

ypical prison, built by Bel-
ians, in which American
nd Belgian hostages were
eld. *(UPI)*

still in his twenties, he set out to educate himself for leadership. And he was unusually successful.

As one who had grown up in the city, who was a part of the Congo's developing middle class (the "elite" or *evolue*), Lumumba was unusually equipped to discuss the Congo's problems. Beginning his work while a prisoner of the Belgians (for embezzlement), Lumumba prepared a manuscript which he submitted to a Belgian publisher in 1956 (he was 31 years of age at the time). The manuscript contained a blueprint for a new Congo.

The publisher wasn't interested, but held the manuscript. But a year after Lumumba's death, when he had become a world figure, the manuscript was published. Too late to change history, the book now is interesting mainly to illustrate the moderate position Patrice Lumumba held a mere four or five years before Congo's independence.

In his reasoned plea to the Belgians, Lumumba asked for prison reform. He discussed the differing effects of imprisonment on the Congolese and on Europeans. He appealed to the Belgians for a more just system of village courts.

He decried the Congolese habits of drinking too much, and smoking hemp (a form of narcotic); the Congolese male's despotic authority over his wife. (Gladys Smithwick, M.D., Free Methodist missionary, describes the condition of Congolese women in these words: "Two African men who lived in a mission area were talking about Christianity and a future life. 'Will there be any women in Heaven?' asked one. 'I don't think so,' came the thoughtful reply. 'There'll be no wood to cut or water to carry, so we won't need them.' ")

The filth and debasement of detribalized communities were evidently as distasteful to Lumumba as they were to Belgians. Education seemed a good part of the answer to him, and he expressed appreciation for the men and women who were giving their lives to educate the Congolese.

But Lumumba did not consider the Belgians blameless for the situations he deplored. "Can it be that colonization has led to a loosening of standards?" he asked, then explained what he meant.

"Theft, for instance, was rare before the arrival of the Europeans. You could close your house with a piece of string and go off on a journey lasting several weeks without fear of anyone breaking in. I believe that the new needs created by civilization, and the difficulties of obtaining what is required for subsistence, are the main causes of theft. The same applies to prostitution. . . . Prostitution seems to be the price paid for civilization; we do not know how it can be successfully eradicated.

"You do not find girls selling their services in the country villages as is the case in towns. . . .

"The Europeans who are in contact with the Congolese outside working hours are generally the less reliable sort who frequent the Congolese quarters with no good motives or, to put the matter briefly and frankly, to get what they can out of it; to go drinking in the bars where beer costs less than in European cafes, and to establish relations with Congolese friends with the object of procuring women at a reduced rate, women whom they almost invariably abandon when they become mothers.

"In the native township these 'doubtful characters' are warmly welcomed by the Congolese, who are pleased and proud to be visited by their seniors and friends. . . . For the majority of Congolese, everything brought by the European, the bearer of civilization, is *good* and *fine*."

And what of the other Europeans, the ones Lumumba respected?

They "rarely frequent the Congolese quarters. This is not from any feeling of contempt — in fact some of them are beginning to frequent these districts — but because they have no particular reason or motive for going there. They cannot go into the African township in the evening just for the fun of going unless they have a *purpose*. Neither can an African go into the European quarter in the evening unless he has some reason or motive for going. Why then should we ask others to do what we cannot do ourselves?

"Hence I do not see how we can condemn these Europeans for not visiting the native areas. Perhaps they ought to go there in groups like tourists or welfare workers, stroll along the roads of the township, shake the hands of passersby, and organize propaganda processions in support of interracial relations. . . .

"There is no law or principle which requires one man to like another."

In another place, where he was appealing for labor reforms, Lumumba criticized some Europeans for "a superiority complex in their relations with the Africans, a complex created not by the color of their skin, but simply and solely by their superior economic position."

L. Arden Almquist, M.D., present director of the Board of Missions of the Evangelical Covenant Church, former missionary in the Congo (whose place on the field was taken by Paul Carlson, M.D.), writes of his own reaction to situations in which he was involved as a young missionary in 1952. His words add perspective to Lumumba's criticism of the European attitude of superiority:

I am going to try to recover the sense of shock which I felt as a missionary novice entering the then Belgian Congo for the first time. I shall do so by describing some typical scenes depicting white-black relations, some of these from the European community, others from the missionary community. I am convinced that the fundamental factor behind current missionary frustration is one of communication, and that the legacy of the past from which we operate — a legacy in part revealed by the scenes I describe — is a more significant element in our difficulty than generally realized.

Scene 1. We arrive in Leopoldville. One is struck by the splendor of the European sector — better than that known by most Belgians in Brussels or Antwerp — and the relative squalor of the African sector. True, there are no separate fountains marked *"blanc"* and *"noir"* — Europeans don't drink water! But in the stores and at the post offices the whites are served first and the Africans made to wait.

Scene 2. We board the Reine Astrid for our trip up-country on the Congo River. The Africans are housed below the Europeans in miserably small rooms with no provisions for eating en route. Everyone brings along such food as he can and buys along the way from such vendors as he encounters at the infrequent stops. The European staterooms above, on the other hand, are ample, there is cuisine, space for lounging on the deck, and some facilities for entertainment.

Scene 3. We are guests at the local Belgian administrator's home. In the course of the evening's conversation, we are offered advice on white-black relations: "These people are all children . . . You can't joke with these people — Africans have no sense of humor . . . Always preserve your dignity." Later I was to visit our dispensary up the river at the village of Ndolanga. In a moment of exuberance inspired by the spontaneous reception accorded me, I balanced a chair on my chin, juggled some oranges, "skinned the cat" on a tree branch and hung from it by my toes. The Congolese were utterly delighted and howled with glee, and from that moment I belonged to that village.

Scene 4. We are having coffee with the local sanitary agent. An African clerk of unusual talent appears for a moment to ask me about his wife, who is a patient at our hospital. When he leaves, I comment on his remarkable qualities. The white man agrees, adding wistfully, "I wish we had more men like him — he's almost white." And then, "But you know, I wouldn't think of asking Andrew into my home!"

Scene 5. A local African chief calls on me one day. At his appearance we extend our right hands and shake warmly. He looks at me a moment and then says, "That's what's different about you missionaries. You shake hands with us."

Scene 6. We are making a long journey, heading for a missionary committee meeting. The three missionaries ride in the cab of the truck in front, and the African passengers in the rear, a motley assortment of people who have sought rides and managed to wear our resistance down to the point of acquiescence . . . The road is hot and dusty. We stop for a bite of lunch along the way. We missionaries take out our Thermos bottles, while the Africans — if they have brought anything — saunter down the road a pace to unroll the leaves from their "kwanga" or nibble at a banana. We arrive at our destination. The Africans help us unload the truck and carry in our paraphernalia. We sit down to supper as a missionary group, served by a 40-50 year-old "boy," who is summoned for his services by a little bell in reach of the hostess.

Scene 7. We are giving the grand tour of the Mission to a visiting Norwegian missionary. It is mid-afternoon, and the mission workmen are seated outside their huts after having had their daily bath, following the cessation of their day's work. They are drinking coffee, and the two white men are offered a cup. I accept mine, served in a glass, very black, and syrupy from too much sugar. The Norwegian refuses his with a *"Non, merci!"* and turns to me, saying, "Surely you don't drink with these people? Aren't you concerned about getting dysentery?"

Scene 8. There is a strike at the Wasolo station. It began with the dismissal of some student nurses. Soon the solidarity of the African community manifests itself. The workmen quit working, and all building ceases. The school teachers send the 200 children home. It is my fault: I had injured the Africans' keen sense of justice in a gesture of anger. The senior missionary on the station tells me, "This is your problem. You handle it." Humbled after thoughtful prayer, I take a can of powdered coffee and some sacks of sugar and go to the African village down the hill where the strikers, in a sullen mood, are sitting around. I tell them I am sorry, ask them to add hot water to the symbols of reconciliation in my hands, and invite them to share a cup of hot coffee with me and talk things over. There are murmurs of surprise, and suddenly there is joy. We drink together, and are friends again. Then someone says, "You are the first white man who ever apologized to us."

Scene 9. I am in my second term. Again we are on a long journey, and I am at the wheel. We are pushing hard and overtake a rickety truck pouring out black exhaust which mingles with the dust of the road. We are in a hurry and hate the dust and smoke and delay. I honk the horn to ask for the road. The driver, an African, doesn't yield, and I lean on the horn as we follow the truck with increasing exasperation. Finally, after ten miles or so, he stops at a village. I pull up alongside him and "eat him out," rejecting in no uncertain terms his simple insistence that he hadn't heard us. When I cooled down later, it was to admit that he was doubtless speaking the truth, and that I had been an ugly fool and a miserable witness to the saving grace of Christ. I have yearned deeply to meet that man again and apologize for my rudeness, but I have never seen him again.

It is difficult to assess the effects of such a system on a man of Lumumba's spirit and drive.

In 1958, Patrice Lumumba formed the first Congolese supra-tribal nationalist movement, the *Mouvement National Congo-lais*. Its purpose was to secure independence. Lumumba's determination was strengthened by the first All-Africa Conference in Ghana, held that same year, which he attended.

He returned to the Congo from that conference prepared to stand against the chiefs who wanted tribal autonomy. Lumumba was now convinced that what the Congo needed was a strong central government.

For the last two years of his life, Lumumba was what Colin Legum (in the Foreword to *Congo, My Country*) calls "the visionary committed to a single idea." Mr. Legum gives three quotations from Lumumba that indicate this:

"For the people, I have no past, no parents, no family. I am an idea . . ."

"I have no right to sleep as long as the people are not masters of their own destiny."

"I am the Congo, the Congo has made me. I am making the Congo."

In the wake of riots in Leopoldville and elsewhere during

1959, the Belgian government granted independence to the Congo in 1960. Patrice Lumumba's political party won the most seats in the legislature, and he was elected the first prime minister. Joseph Kasavubu, leader of the opposition, was chosen president.

From the beginning, Lumumba's government was in trouble. Many of the problems antedated independence, for Belgian rule had been permitted to grow progressively weaker throughout the country. Anarchy had already commenced in isolated instances where leadership to replace the Belgians was inadequate.

Many Belgians left the Congo immediately after independence. At first the exodus consisted mainly of women and children, which unfortunately contributed to the crisis. According to Congolese folk tradition (which is, of course, shared by most of the world), this was interpreted as preparation for war.

An exodus of men from government service and the companies soon followed, which eased the fear of war. But this left much of the country and its industry in untrained Congolese hands. Without preparation, the nationals could not possibly take over the positions that were abandoned.

Ralph Bunche, United Nations representative, blamed Belgium for many of the Congo's troubles, saying that it had failed to prepare and educate the Congolese before independence.

The makeup of the government itself reflected this lack of preparation. Of the top 23 men, all but four were of the clerk level (a bit broader than the term implies), in civil service or the companies. Only one was university-trained.

But the Congolese were not merely untrained; they were naive in what they expected after independence. Their childlike anticipation created a great problem for Lumumba, since he could not possibly provide good housing, high pay, automobiles and many other advantages previously possessed by the Belgians. Disillusionment was bound to result.

In *Force Publique*, the national army, disappointment was keen when a Belgian general continued to lead, and Congolese soldiers were not immediately promoted to officer rank. Lumumba saw the need for time and training — "It is not because the Congo is independent that we can turn a private into a general," he said.

This response to their demands infuriated the soldiers: "Mr. Lumumba judges us incapable of taking the place of the officers. . . . Dear Lumumba, friend of the Europeans, we guarantee you the ruination of your powers and of your Congo so long as you insult us as ignorant people who are incapable of taking the places of your white brothers."

The statement was prophetic, for more than any other factor, the mutiny of his troops was probably the prime reason for Lumumba's downfall.

In an attempt to regain the ground he had lost, Lumumba announced the removal of Belgian General Janssens, and the promotion of all troops one rank. But this did not satisfy the soldiers. And the substitution of Congolese for Belgian officers was unsatisfactory for another reason, which may have been a major factor in the mutiny. Tribal loyalties continued strong, even in the army. And when, in the course of promotions, a member of an inferior tribe was placed in authority over others who considered their tribe superior, they refused to obey the new officer. This break in the chain of command was disastrous to discipline in the army.

Less than a month after independence came to the Congo, the Congolese national army (*Force Publique*) mutinied. Since the *Force* combined both army and police functions, the result was destructive. Premier Moise Tshombe of Katanga declared the independence of his province from the national government, and Premier Albert Kalonji followed with a declaration of independence for Southern Kasai Province.

Faced with a country that seemed to be falling apart during its first month of independent life, Lumumba appealed to the United Nations for military aid to restore order. At the same time, the Belgian government reversed its withdrawal of troops, doubtless to protect Belgian citizens rather than to recover the Congo as a colony. There is little doubt that Lumumba did not believe this, but considered Belgian forces in the Congo a threat to its independent life at that time.

When U.N. troops arrived, Lumumba found that he was not in command. United Nations policy was to support the unity of the country, but not to put down the secessionist governments of Katanga and Kasai.

Lumumba failed to see, or at least failed to admit, that the objective of the U.N. force in the Congo was different from the objective of his own government. His great disenchantment with the U.N. and the West seems to have come when he found that neither Ralph Bunche nor Dag Hammarskjöld intended to subdue the rebellion in Katanga and Katai, restoring central government to the Congo. Instead, they conceived the U.N.'s purpose in the Congo to be one of preventing the spread of conflict and the involvement of major world powers. Their authority came from the Security Council and General Assembly of the U.N., to which they were responsible for their actions, rather than from the Lumumba government.

Mr. Hammarskjöld's great fear was that the Congo would become another Korea. He spoke of "efforts from all sides to make the Congo a happy hunting ground for national interests." He further said: "For seven or eight months, through efforts far beyond the imagination of those who founded this organization, [the U.N.] has tried to counter tendencies to introduce the big-power conflicts into Africa and put the young African countries under the shadow of the cold war."

The United States fully supported Dag Hammarskjöld and the United Nations' limited involvement. Russia did not. Therefore Patrice Lumumba turned to the Communist bloc of nations for help, and he was not disappointed.

The Russians immediately supplied a limited number of airplanes and trucks. In *Africa's Red Harvest*, Pieter Lessing documents other Communist support pledged and provided. Lumumba's defiance of the United Nations made him a ready instrument for their purposes. Communist Eastern Europe supplied guns, which later found their way into the hands of Simbas. China promised financial aid (actually not given, because before the aid could arrive, Lumumba was captured and murdered, and his government had collapsed).

Encouraged by the Communist bloc of nations, Lumumba determined to make his own attempt to overthrow the secessionist governments of Kasai and Katanga. He started with Kasai, and had a small group of hand-picked troops under General Victor Lundula flown there in Russian planes. The attempt to subdue the rebellion was abortive, but thousands of Baluba tribespeople were killed in the brief fighting. This action by Lumumba's troops was particularly offensive to Mr. Hammarskjöld, who described it as having "the characteristics of the crime of genocide."

From this brief military engagement, Lumumba reaped alienation from many Congolese who had formerly supported him, and the undying hatred of the Baluba tribe.

Angered by Lumumba's private deal with the Russians, President Kasavubu dismissed him as prime minister after he had served less than ten weeks. (According to the Congo Constitution, the president had this authority.) Lumumba resisted the action, but in a brief period of time the government was overthrown by the Congo army, led by Colonel Joseph Mobutu. Lumumba fled and, according to Colin Legum, had to make funeral arrangements at this time for his child who had died in Geneva. He was soon captured.

A new government was formed, with Antoine Gizenga, former deputy prime minister, as Lumumba's successor. Two months later, President Kasavubu formed another government, ending military rule. Joseph Ileo became the third prime minister in eight months.

Soon after the new government was formed, the Katanga government announced that Patrice Lumumba had been killed by tribespeople. An investigation by the United Nations implicated Moise Tshombe in the murder.

An editorial in *The New Republic*, "Lumumba's Murder," commented: "Lumumba, for all his obvious faults, was a very human African national whose association with the Soviet Union was pragmatic rather than ideological." In desperation, as a last resort, Lumumba turned to the Communists.

How do we explain Congo's first prime minister?

Patrice Lumumba was an *evolue*, one of the "elite." As a member of this small group of Congolese, he had only limited rapport with the common people, the tribespeople of the country which he was governing.

But if he was removed from those beneath him, he was even more separated from the white, educated people with whom he had daily contact.

Thus he was pressed between two cultures, neither of which he could accept, and in neither of which he could find acceptance.

"In short," says Alan P. Merriam, African research specialist of Northwestern University, "a grade-schooler had been thrown upon the world and had been expected to act like a mature world statesman. It is no wonder that his course seems erratic, for he had no experience to guide him. . . . Let it be understood that Lumumba, if erratic, [was] not a stupid man; witness the speed with which he came to understand at least the superficialities of the East-West struggle and to play one side against the other. And some of his behavior is made clearer if we consider the fact that many Africans genuinely wish to remain uncommitted in the East-West struggle for world dominance. The result of his semi-aggressive neutralist stand, coupled with his rudimentary knowledge of world political ideologies, was that Lumumba was genuinely prepared to take assistance from any source which proffered it, without realizing the consequences. Although we saw him moving into the Russian camp, his move was not necessarily because of a love for communism; probably, it was that in taking proffered Russian unilateral assistance, he saw a way to extricate himself from his difficulties" (*Congo: Background of Conflict*).

Lumumba's murder was exploited by the Communists, who found his memory a useful propaganda instrument. With much fanfare, Russian Communists named a Moscow university for African students for him. His statue was erected in Stanleyville. His name became a rallying cry throughout Africa.

During the four years between Lumumba's death and the Stanleyville events described in this book, the United Nations

Congo force tried to restore order to the newly independent nation. Twenty thousand troops from 34 nations participated in the police action, which cost more than $400 million and took the lives of 200 U.N. soldiers. Another casualty was the United Nations secretary-general, Dag Hammarskjöld, who died in a plane crash on his way to negotiate with secessionist leader Moise Tshombe.

Failing to bring Tshombe to terms, United Nations forces finally drove him into exile. The United States government concurred in this action. But about the time Stanleyville fell to the Rebel army, Moise Tshombe returned to power in the Congo, as premier. He had the backing of the United States in this position. But now he had a secessionist problem of his own, the rebellion in northeast Congo led by Christophe Gbenye. Hatred for Tshombe by the pro-Lumumba forces, including Communists, was a factor in the bitterness of sub-sequent fighting.

At the outset of the Rebel action, the United States pro-vided only a small amount of aid, both money and supplies, to Tshombe's government. Moise Tshombe recognized the need for white officers in his national army, because of the continuing lack of Congolese trained for leadership and their refusal to serve under leaders of tribes other than their own. And so he advertised for white recruits in other African na-tions, and built the "mercenary" army. This white element in the national army further increased Rebel bitterness and also stirred sympathy for the Rebel cause on the part of other African nations. But Tshombe's realistic decision to hire white mercenaries was not different from Lumumba's previous action of similar expediency.

Direct American-Belgian intervention became necessary to

protect citizens of these countries after the fall of Stanleyville. But the two countries entered the conflict reluctantly, aware of the advantage thus provided Communist propagandists. Increased danger to the white prisoners was another necessary concomitant of the decision.

Intervention consisted of the 600 men of Belgium's crack Para-Commando regiment, flown into the Congo in 14 United States-piloted C-130 planes.

For the observer, the surprising thing is not that the United States government intervened, but that intervention was so late and so limited. It is indicative of the delicate balance of world peace, and the fear of war, that a major government should stand by while its citizens — let alone its State Department representatives — are imprisoned, tortured and killed. The Congo affair, on top of other similar incidents of recent years, must of necessity foster insecurity among American missionaries and business representatives — as well as members of embassies and consulates — on overseas assignments.

A new dimension of danger seems to have entered today's foreign service. The days when a major power mobilized to protect one citizen, anchoring gunboats offshore or dispatching an army, are past. The citizen overseas must now reckon with the fact that he is largely on his own.

Any assessment of deterioration in the Congo since independence was granted by Belgium in 1960 must avoid the mistake of blaming Belgium. It is true that the Belgians lagged behind the British, for instance, in educating nationals and preparing a cadre of Congolese for responsible leadership. But they recognized this and had embarked upon a program to close the gap within a few years, when world opinion — including the United States — brought pressure to bear upon Belgium to divest itself of this colony and grant immediate independence. Belgium's hand was forced, and the Free World suffered. The Congo itself suffered most.

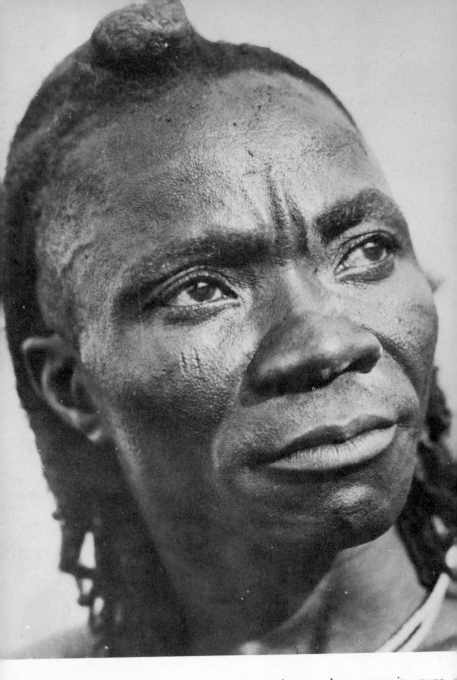

CONGO TRIBESMEN shown here and on opposite page
Bambala (above), Nkundu woman (top left), Bapende (t
right), Baluba (bottom left) and Wagenia (bottom righ
(UPI)

5/Humiliation

"DAVIS, WHAT HAPPENED after your wife and children were taken away from you at the airport?"

It was now dark in Stanleyville. Outside Hotel des Chutes, lights were coming on; Simba guards in the street below could be distinguished by their glowing cigarettes and the occasional striking of a match.

"They threw me back in the women's toilet. Then the Simbas ordered us to take off all our clothes except our shorts."

"Hoyt and the consular staff, too?"

"All six of us. They took our clothes away and then threw them in the slop that was on the floor. I think I told you this afternoon, when we were talking about it, what a mess the place was — the toilets had overflowed."

"What was their idea?"

"Same old thing. Humiliate us. Show us that they were the boss. They made wild statements about us, they hit us with the backsides of their bayonets, they threw solids from the toilet overflow at us. They seemed to want to make us feel as low as possible."

"How did you feel?"

"Too scared to feel low or anything else just then."

"But how did you feel as a — well, as a *Christian*? After all, you are a missionary. Did you feel persecuted?" Dr. Mare-scotti pressed the point.

"I guess I did think about being in this mess because of the Gospel — I was suffering for the Gospel's sake, not for political reasons like the rest. But actually, I didn't do a lot of thinking. I just took each moment as it came."

"Is this really suffering because of your religion?"

"Yes, I think so. The Apostle Paul suffered sometimes be-cause he was caught in the crosscurrents of political involve-ment. Of course, he also suffered for religious reasons, but politics was there, in the background."

"The same thing was true of Christ."

"Sure."

"How long did they keep you there in the toilet room?"

"Until later that night. Then the commandant came in and said we'd have to pay a hundred-thousand francs each for our release. [Equivalent: about $250 each.] Michael Hoyt agreed right away."

"Did they let you go then?"

"No, although they did let us sleep in the hallway that night, outside the toilet area. Not that it was much better — the floor was flooded there, too. But at least we had room to lie down in, which was better than the night before, according to Hoyt. This was their second night there, you know."

"The American consular staff has really been through it."

"They sure have. The next afternoon — Sunday — they moved us to a Sabena Airlines residence across the street. It was sort of a motel cottage for transient guests, one room with a bath. What an improvement! Our morale picked up immediately."

"How long did they keep you there?"

"A little over two weeks."

"Did they have the place guarded?"

"Yes, there were Simbas outside the door. We felt sort of insecure because we never knew what was going to happen. And the fact that we didn't speak Swahili didn't help. You know that I'd only been in the Congo for about four months when this happened, so I hadn't more than begun to learn the language."

"And Michael Hoyt had only been around this area a short time — wasn't it three weeks? — when the storm broke. So he was unfamiliar with Swahili, too."

"In a way, it's one of those unfortunate things that Klingerman left when he did. He really knew this part of the Congo. I understand Hoyt is only on a temporary assignment here."

"Some assignment it's turned out to be!"

"It was even more discouraging for the three communications men who had worked for the consulate. They didn't consider themselves politicians like the State Department people. They had come to do a job, and they didn't feel that they belonged in prison. So they just thought about their families and their other responsibilities outside Congo."

"How were you fed during those two weeks?"

"The Sabena Airlines employees often brought food across the road to us. And Michael Hoyt's servant was allowed to bring us some meals from the consulate. So we didn't starve."

"Was it after that when you were taken to Central Prison?"

"Yes, around the fifth of September. It was a Saturday night. All the consuls in Stanleyville had been invited to a meeting with Gbenye. Well, at the last minute Hoyt and his assistant were told that they were going, too. They weren't told until a quarter-to-five — I remember that they only had fifteen minutes to get dressed and over to the president's residence. Well, when they arrived, the British consul and the rest were all inside. Just as they were about to enter, General Olenga drove up. He was furious to see them waiting to go in. He said they should never have been invited. So he rushed them back to the Sabena residence, where they picked the rest of us up and took us all to Central Prison. That was the end of our plush living for a while."

"I know. I was in Central Prison for a short time myself."

"What's it like?"

"Our cell was about 12 by 15 feet. The ceiling was about 12 feet off the floor. There was one door opening on a central courtyard, and a window faced that way. Another window — that one was barred — was in the outside wall, facing the street. Both windows were about nine feet off the floor. The mosquitoes were really fierce at night, and flies during the daytime. It was really crawling. But I only had to put up with Central Prison for two days — on September seventh I was released."

"How about Hoyt and the others?"

"No, they had to stay. It happened like this. General Olenga came that particular day to pardon 40 to 50 Simba prisoners who were also in Central Prison, so they could rejoin the troops. They were in prison for various offenses. So on the way out, after he had finished this job, he stopped in front of us Americans. He looked straight at me and asked me one question: 'Are you the American missionary?' I said I was, and he told his soldiers to take me off to the side. He said some more things that I couldn't understand, but later someone told me what they were. He said the missionary was a good fellow, what was he doing here, and 'I don't want you soldiers bothering the missionary.' Then he really harrangued Hoyt and the other consular men."

"Did they just turn you loose?"

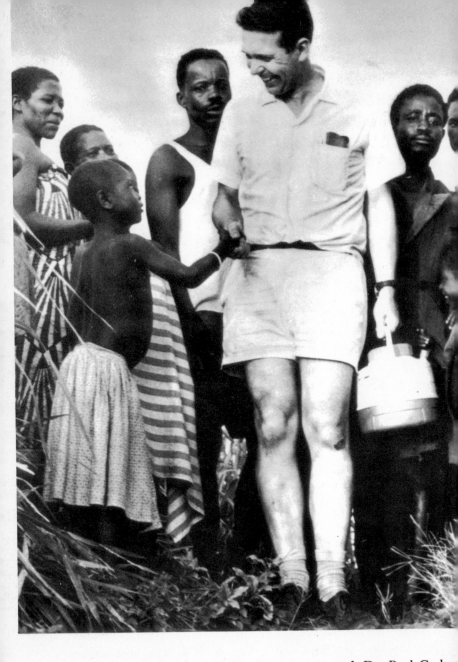

FOUR MONTHS before he was executed, Dr. Paul Carlso[n]
happily welcomed by Congo villagers to whom he brou[ght]
medical help and the Christian message. *(Smith Klin[e &]
French)*

"They would have, but I insisted on having some guards to take me to the LECO headquarters. It's just across the street, but I wasn't going to take any chances on being arrested and brought back to prison, or something else happening. Incidentally, after General Olenga said I was a good fellow, and he didn't want them to bother me, the Simbas couldn't do enough for me.

"So they took me across the street and I yelled up at a window, 'Mr. Kinso!' I was about the only missionary who called him that — the rest just called him Kinso — and so he knew right away who was there. He came running down, and we just hugged each other. It was wonderful to see him."

"Kinso has surely been a tower of strength in these weeks." Al Larson, usually silent while Chuck was telling his story to the rest, spoke with deep respect of the missionary who had first come to the Congo in 1921.

"I suppose it was a real disappointment when Kinso told you that your wife and children had already gone out to Kilometer 8."

"It sure was. I wanted to go right out there, and so I tried to get the Simbas to take me. But they said there wasn't any car available, and I certainly didn't want to hike out there alone. So I spent the night with Kinso, and the next day I found my way out to Kilometer 8 with an English missionary."

"That's where you were then — at Kilometer 8 — until they picked you up the other day and brought you in here?"

"Yes, I was there with my wife and children for about two months. Del Carper and Al Larson were there, too, until they picked us up. We've all left our families out there."

6/Kilometer 8

OUT IN THE COUNTRY, about five miles beyond the limits of Stanleyville, was a mission station everyone referred to as Kilometer 8. (If concentric circles were drawn on a map, with Stanleyville at the center, this location would be one of the points eight kilometers from the city.)

A dirt road went past the front of the mission property. Simba soldiers — Lions — often marched down this road during those uneasy months late in 1964.

The main building was a large stone house, once owned by Belgians. Beside it was a cinder-block building, sometimes called the Hangar. During peaceful days, the Hangar had housed African pastors during spiritual life conferences. It contained five bedrooms.

A short distance away was a little collection of cottages, where the five houseboys who were employed at the mission station lived with their families.

Behind the whole property was the tropical forest — dense, forbidding, with undergrowth that seemed to grow back together even before the machete had finished cutting its path.

Hemmed in by Lions at the front, and the jungle at the rear, a small group of missionaries and their children — about 24 — lived through the difficult and dangerous weeks at Kilometer 8.

It was here that Muriel Davis and her children found refuge after they had stayed with the Jenkinsons in Stanleyville for two weeks. The British consul arranged the move, "so your children will have more room to play." But there were other reasons that he didn't mention: the situation in Stanleyville was becoming even more tense, and the facilities of LECO were increasingly strained by other refugees.

Now, more than ever before, Kilometer 8 was needed by the missionaries. It was close enough to Stanleyville for wives to keep in touch with their imprisoned husbands, and for news to reach them of what was going on. From Kilometer 8 they could also send word to their husbands. But it was far enough out to be under less pressure, at least in the early weeks.

And it was to Kilometer 8 that Chuck Davis came a few days later, and remained for the next two months.

Until his arrest with the other Americans, Reverend Al Larson was in charge of Kilometer 8. He was senior missionary of the Unevangelized Fields Mission. His wife, Jean, and their two-year-old daughter were also at Kilometer 8.

Hector McMillan and Bob McAllister were the two men at the station during almost this whole time. Even before the uprising, Hector and Ione had made the station an oasis for missionaries from their own and other societies. Everyone felt at home with the McMillans. They had six sons, ranging from ten to seventeen years of age, with them at the station.

The McAllisters had three children at the station, while Del and Lois Carper had a daughter. (Del was also later imprisoned in Stanleyville with Al Larson and Chuck Davis.) Mrs. M. Southard and her son, and the Misses Viola Walker, Mina Erskine and Olive Bjerkseth completed the group.

When the crisis came, authorities at the schools for missionaries' children had closed their doors, thinking that the students would be safer in their parents' custody. For this reason, the number of children at Kilometer 8 was unusually large.

During the early weeks of house arrest, the missionaries maintained a semblance of missionary work, always under the Simbas' eyes. Ione McMillan and Mina Erskine were called upon to help in nursing, especially in difficult childbirths, at nearby villages. They rode bicycles for the trips.

But the children were a problem, especially as one uneventful day followed another. They soon tired of the restricted life and activities at the station, but with Simbas frequently in the area, they could not be permitted freedom of movement.

And so, after the parents had prayed, they decided that school should be organized and carried on each weekday. Lois Carper and Viola Walker taught classes from 8:30 a.m. to 12 noon, then from 1:30 to 3:30 p.m. Olive Bjerkseth taught the older children French. Ione McMillan taught kindergarten.

The children were also given work assignments. They picked weevils out of the wheat before it was ground for flour. The older boys made cement blocks for a new building, under Hector's supervision.

This combination of study and work kept the children busy. It also preserved their morale during increasingly worrisome days.

For all four Davises, Kilometer 8 was a welcome refuge. In the four months since they arrived in the Congo, their lives could scarcely have been more unsettled.

At the time of the Rebel uprising, Charles Davis was 31 years of age. Tall, athletic, with steel-gray eyes set in an angular face, he gives an impression of great intensity. His manner of speaking heightens the impression. Chuck grew up in Roxbury, in a somewhat depressed area of Boston, where his father worked in the Federal Reserve Bank mailroom. After a somewhat wild youth, Chuck was converted and entered Gordon College (Beverly Farms, Massachusetts). His liberal arts education — main interest, philosophy — was followed by three years' study at Gordon Divinity School. At Gordon, Chuck met his wife, who came from the Blue Ridge Mountains of Virginia. After he was graduated from seminary, Chuck worked in a Roanoke, Virginia, store for a short period of time, then accepted the call to become pastor of the Glade Creek Baptist Church in Blue Ridge, Virginia.

But all the while, Chuck and Muriel were directing their lives toward Africa.

"One of the first things that touched my life for foreign missions," Chuck explains, "was the Auca incident. I don't owe my missionary call to it, but it made a deep impression on me. There were five young men, with excellent training, who went willingly into that dangerous situation. [Dietrich] Bonhoeffer says the disciple of Jesus must burn his boat and launch out into the sea of total insecurity, and there he will learn of Jesus. I think he's right — you don't learn of Him when all things are secure, and everything around you is roses and sugar. You learn of Jesus when you're on the firing-line. I don't mean that you have to be on the firing-line out in Congo; you can be on it in New York or Chicago or Toronto. But wherever you are, it's a matter of putting yourself in a potentially dangerous situation. And you can't steer clear of criticism."

Chuck and Muriel were in that dangerous situation from the moment they arrived in the Congo, April 27, 1964, within a few days of the fall of Stanleyville. Banjwadi, the cooperative Bible seminary to which Chuck was appointed by the Africa Inland Mission, is about 40 miles north of Stanleyville. Because of its location, missionaries stationed there were vulnerable to the Rebels' advance. For the first three months, Chuck and Muriel were assigned to study the Swahili language.

It was at Banjwadi that the Davises were first taken into custody by the Rebels. After Chuck's release from Central Prison, they could probably have returned there, but they felt safer at the Unevangelized Fields Mission station near Stanleyville.

Occasionally, Congolese Christians came to Kilometer 8 for advice from Reverend Al Larson, or for help with various problems. Seemingly, they were not afraid of continuing identification with the missionaries.

One teacher who had run out of material for his school came for new supplies. When he arrived, the missionaries were surprised to learn that he had bicycled 30 miles, and was ready to go back immediately — despite the fact that he had been forced to pass 15 or 20 barriers.

"Unless you lived in the Congo at that time," Chuck Davis says, "you can hardly understand what that meant. Each barrier was as close to hell on earth for the Congolese as it could be. The Simbas might beat him, abuse him, open any packages he had with him, steal what they wanted — each Simba was a law unto himself. Yet that teacher went through the treatment 30 or 40 times, counting both ways, just so he'd have materials and wouldn't have to close his school. We were really humbled by such an incredible display of dedication."

Surprisingly, this man was not one the missionaries had expected to stand firm when the pressure was applied, and yet he did. On the other hand, a teacher who seemed to possess the spiritual resources to stand up to anything was one of the two or three Christian teachers from the whole area who joined up with the Simba army.

Church leaders also came to report on Christian activity in

their villages: that the church here was continuing faithful, that they were still having prayer meetings, that they were praying for the missionaries, that pupils had not dropped out of school. Reports of this sort were a great encouragement to Al Larson and the other missionaries at Kilometer 8.

During their two months at the station, Chuck and Muriel, with their two children, lived in a room inside the Hangar. Hector McMillan helped Chuck put a king-sized bed together, and make a crib for the baby. Their two children found much company among the other children and young people at the station.

The Hangar, where the Davis family lived, was about a hundred yards away from the house of a Congolese Christian who worked at the mission station. "The Congolese people love to sing," Chuck explains. "Each night, just before they went to sleep, they sang hymns. We would lie in bed and listen to them. Somehow, in those dark nights, their singing was a ray of light."

One day Steve Davis (then four years old) prayed, "Dear God, please keep the bad Simbas away from us, and take care of Uncle Al [Reverend Al Larson] who is in town today doing some shopping. Don't let the bad Simbas hurt him, and help him get back in time for dinner."

Al did make it back in time for dinner that night.

Muriel tried to impress on her children that there were good Simbas as well as bad ones. "You just can't call a man bad before you know anything about him," she said. "Those Simbas who come here and don't bother us, who go away without doing any harm, they are good Simbas. The ones who come here and make all the racket, and shoot their guns — they're bad Simbas."

One day the propaganda machinery circulated the false report that the Americans had dropped an atomic bomb on a village to the north. According to the report, the bomb had killed six thousand innocent women and children. Two days of mourning were ordered.

"It was interesting to see how Steve and Beth (then two years old) reacted," Muriel says. "We couldn't let them go out and play. But we couldn't just pen them up inside, either. It's hard to keep little children's voices down, and to keep them from sounding happy. If the Simbas heard them laughing, they thought the children were laughing at them. So it was a strain on the women, trying to keep the children from showing excitement or joy — not just those two days of official mourning, when we had to be especially careful, but all the time. We didn't want them to lose their childish happiness and become fearful.

"Well, we tried to keep them inside those two days, so the Simbas wouldn't see them. I remember afterward, Steve and Beth wanted to know if they could laugh again."

Muriel Davis is radiantly beautiful, with the graciousness of her Virginia background, and the guilelessness of some who have known God since childhood. Her eyes impress you: they are lovely and warm and kind. A senior missionary says, "Muriel has the mysterious quality of which martyrs are made. John and Betty Stam [martyred in China] were her examples."

What kept the parents on an even keel during those months? According to Chuck, it was the Bible. "There was never any real relief from the terror that was all around us, except for our times in the Word, reading the Bible. During those three-and-a-half months, I read through the Bible twice. In the Bible I found comfort — the assurance that God had control. The Bible will never be the same to me."

7/"Safari Is Sorrow"

A POINT COMES IN THE HISTORY of today's foreign mission when the work must become "their" work if it is to grow, perhaps even survive.

It can no longer be foreign-centered, whether the foreigners come from the United States, Canada, Great Britain or Germany.

To continue beyond that point is to invite anti-white or anti-foreign, nationalistic trouble. To recognize that point and initiate change is probably today's prime evidence of sanctified missionary statesmanship. And holiness is often more needed than statesman-like qualities.

But God has His ways of forcing change and growth.

In Ethiopia, war with Italy suddenly removed foreign missionaries from the scene. And who, hearing of the growth in the church during those years, can doubt that the Italian invaders were God's instrument to develop an indigenous church.

For China, Communism was the wrath God used to shape His praise.

Charles Davis tells of reading Leslie Lyall's *Come Wind,*

Come Weather while imprisoned in Hotel des Chutes. He wrote this entry in the small notebook in which he put down some of his thoughts and experiences during those days: "Today I'm reading the account of the Communist takeover of the church in China. I am humiliated by the energetic, courageous stand of men like Pastor Wang Ming-tao.

"In October, 1956, one young Chinese was offered release if only he would stop praying — which was called an evidence of an unbalanced mind. But he preferred to stay in prison and pray."

Leslie Lyall describes, on the basis of available information (in 1960), the persecution of Christians, and the Communist government's attempt to mold the church to its own ends. Compromise there was, sin and failure of Christians (including some leaders), but against the dark backdrop are the shining indications that God was continuing to build His church in China, in the midst of the storm.

And so it has been in the Congo. Christians have stood up to the Lions, and some have fled. As in China, some joined the Lions, denying the faith; others denied the missionaries. (Even the giant Pastor Wang Ming-tao had his breaking-point, which he later confessed with tears.)

Here is the testimony of a Congolese pastor, telling what happened to him during the time Chuck was imprisoned at Hotel des Chutes, and Muriel was at Kilometer 8. For his protection in the shifting political situation, his name is withheld. But his name is known to God and the Africa Inland Mission, to whom his faithfulness in spite of suffering is as precious as is the faithfulness of their British and American missionaries.

I am telling you about the troubles I had with the Simbas.
The one who made the first accusation against us was Yosefa.

He accused us before the Simba leaders, saying that we had a radio transmitter at the mission. On Wednesday the Simbas came in trucks and surrounded the whole mission compound. At the time, I was reading my Bible in my house.

When I saw that they had surrounded the mission, I came out of my house with my Bible in my hand.

They said, "Who are you?"

I replied that I was the pastor.

"Where is the owner of that house?" the leader demanded, pointing to another house.

"When he heard that you had arrived in the area, he fled with his wife and children to the bush," I replied.

Then he asked for the school director and the other pastor. I told him that they were both absent, the pastor at a nearby village, while the school director had gone to reopen a school in accordance with Simba instructions.

They then demanded that I open the door of my house, which I did. Inside, they made a thorough inspection, looking into boxes, above the ceiling — everywhere. But they found nothing except a picture of President Kasavubu.

They asked why I had such a picture in my house and I explained that it belonged to my children, who had left it in a suitcase in my house with other things.

"You are a liar. You are a member of the P.N.P. [opposition party]. Today you will become butter [a slang way of saying you will die]."

Finding no radio transmitter in my house, they went to the other house, where they broke down the door and made a thorough search. They found no transmitter, but they did find a list of 25 soldiers.

I told them that I knew nothing about the list, that it was found in another man's house, but they insisted that I produce those 25 men. I told them this was impossible.

Then they made a thorough search of all the other houses, the church and the school buildings. But they found nothing. So they said to me, "Today you will become butter because you have hidden 25 soldiers, and you have a picture of President Kasavubu. You are a P.N.P. and today you will die."

They put me into a truck and took me across the way to the Simba colonel, where they reported, "We found this pastor, but none of the others were there. We searched his house and found nothing except this picture of Kasavubu; but in his neighbor's house we found this list of soldiers with the numbers of their guns."

The colonel was very angry and said, "Take him outside and question him for ten minutes, and if he does not confess the matter of the transmitter too, he will die."

So they took me out on the porch. An adjutant came with paper and pencil to write down what I said. He warned me that the colonel had given me only ten minutes to confess everything, and if that were not done, I would become butter. So he said, "Let's start with the transmitter."

I answered him, "Before God, and before you, adjutant, I declare that we never had a transmitter at our mission."

He looked at me closely and said, "Your eyes look like a person who is not telling the truth. Tell me everything."

So I repeated what I had already said, that the mission had no transmitter.

"If your mission had no radio," he asked, "how did your missionaries talk to their friends on other stations?"

"Being in town, our missionaries used the government telegraph services."

He asked again and again, but each time I insisted that our mission had no transmitter.

Then he left the matter of the transmitter and asked why I had a picture of President Kasavubu in my house. I explained, as I had to the soldiers, that it was among some things of my children, who were going to school in Stanleyville.

So he said, "Good. And why did you have the list of soldiers?"

When I explained that the list was found in my neighbor's house, not in mine, he began to read the names. As he read, some of the other Simbas overheard and came running, saying, "I know that man. He was in Stanleyville and turned Simba." "I know that one, he's with us here." And so it went down the list. When all had been identified, he left.

He came back because the ten minutes wasn't up yet, and once more I protested that I knew nothing of any radio transmitter.

"You are a liar. Bring me a rope."

Two men came with the rope and made me lie down on the cement floor. Then they beat me with guns. After this they tied my hands behind my back, tied my feet together, and pulled them up to meet my hands.

"My God, help me! My God, help me!" I cried out.

They scoffed, "Call on your God. We have killed many and their Gods have not helped them. You and your God have done very badly, because you connived with your missionaries to call for the Americans to come and fight against us, and to take away our land. You pastors have done very badly. Your white people have taught you very bad politics, and today you will die."

I told them, "If I die for the name of Jesus, it is no great matter."

So they got water in a pail, and pushed my head into the water, two people pushing my head and one man holding the pail.

I thrashed about. The water went into my nose, my ears, my chest; and when I was about to die, and was lying still, they took my head out of the pail and poured the water over my whole body.

The colonel had been watching this, and when I could see again, he came over with a knife in his hand, saying, "Tell the truth as you know it in your heart."

"Before God, and before you, colonel, I declare that there has never been a transmitter at our mission."

When he heard this, he was furious. "This knife has killed many people, people who were greater and more important than you! Even though you have denied everything, this knife has killed many people! If you deny that you have a transmitter, you shall become butter!"

So I told him, "Even though I die for the sake of the Lord Jesus, it is not a great matter."

He was quiet for a time. Then he asked, "Do you have a wife and children?"

"I have seven children, but my wife is dead."

"Where are your seven children?"

"They live with me."

He thought for a time, then ordered that I be untied. My hands and feet were so numb that I could not stand, so two Simba soldiers held me up. He ordered that I be put into solitary confinement until a decision should be made the next day.

So they took me away to prison where they put me in a cell that was so filthy with water and human excrement that I could not sleep that night. Since my birth, I had never been in prison; nor had I been beaten or whipped by the State. But this day I learned about this bitterness at the hands of the Simbas.

I was in prison four days, and I thought they had forgotten about me. Friday they did not come. Saturday they did not come. Sunday they did not come. But Monday was the day of a big celebration and parade, and no doubt this was to be the day of our execution.

At 11 o'clock Monday, a large truck filled with Simbas came to the prison and surrounded it. They ordered all of us prisoners into the truck, 19 of us — all civilians. The chef de poste began to call the roll. While we were answering our names, an adjutant came hurrying up from the monument on a motorcycle.

"Why are you wasting your time calling names?" he demanded. "The colonel is waiting at the monument. Hurry! Go to the monument at once. Chauffeur, safari!"

The chauffeur stepped on the starter, but the engine refused to turn over. He tried again. Nothing happened. They began to push the truck, but still it wouldn't go.

So they unloaded us and lined us up in a column, by two's, and began to hurry us to the monument. Two prisoners and a Simba soldier, two prisoners and a Simba soldier.

At the crossroad to the airport, we met the colonel, who was coming to get us. He turned around and waited for us at the police station. We were running along the road, *kpa, kpa, kpa,* until we came in front of him.

"Halt!" he said. We stopped. We were very tired.

"Men from Mahagi," he said, "step out." No one moved. "Men from Djugu, step out." No one moved. "Men from Mangbwalo!" No one. These were prisoners from other towns who had been brought to Lumumba for execution before the monument.

Everyone was trembling, no one was able to move.

When the colonel saw that no one moved, he divided us into two groups, like the Bible says in Matthew 25:33. When the Lord Jesus comes again, He will divide the people, the sheep from the goats. So the colonel divided us, one-two, one-two, one-two, until he came to the last man.

"All of you on the left hand, go to the monument. Those on the right hand, go back to prison."

I was in the right-hand group.

Eight Simbas took the unfortunate ten to the monument for execution; four took the rest of us back to prison.

When we were nearly to the prison, some other Simbas saw that we were returning. So they began to collect rocks, clubs and guns, and waited for us at the prison door. When we arrived, they locked the door and began to beat us until blood ran to the cement like it was nothing. Later they unlocked the doors and let us enter the prison, sending each one of us to his cell.

We lay utterly still, exhausted, for an hour. Then I saw that five brother prisoners had gathered around me. There were two Babiras, a Mumbissa, a Mungiti and an Alur. They all came to me and said, "Pastor, what shall we do about this matter? What shall we do?"

"Brethren, there is nothing else to do," I replied. "They have already done in the other men. Only we remain. We don't know but that tomorrow we shall die, too. So we must do as the Bible says in Amos 4:12, 'Prepare to meet your God.'

"So the only thing for you to do is to be ready to meet your God tomorrow, or even today. In Luke 23:42, the thief on the cross, when he saw that his hour had come, said to the Lord Jesus, 'Lord, remember me when You come into Your kingdom.' And Jesus replied, 'Today you shall be with me in paradise.' The thief settled his affairs there on the cross, when he was about to die, and you here in prison must make your peace with God.

"As for me, I can meet my Lord with joy. The only sorrow of my heart is because of my children. If the mother dies, it is good that the father be left to care for the children; and if the father dies, that the mother be left. For both to leave on safari is sorrow, and that is why I sorrow for my children.

Rebeka has already died and I am dying. But in my heart I have joy."

One of them said, "But pastor, I am a Roman Catholic. What shall I do?"

"Don't think of the matter of being a Roman Catholic," I replied. "Roman Catholic is a name; Protestant is a name; but the One who died on the cross to save us from our sins is the Lord Jesus Christ, whom God the Father gave to redeem us. Trust *Him*. He Himself said, 'I am the true way to Heaven. Nobody comes to the Father except by Me.'"

When I finished saying this, they began to confess their sins one by one before God. When they had finished, we knelt there in the filthy prison cell and prayed to God. Then they returned to their cells.

At two o'clock in the afternoon, we heard a truck arrive in front of the prison, and we thought they had come to take us out to die. But it was a messenger who had come.

"Where are the prisoners who were returned this morning?"

The chef de poste said that we were in the stronghold.

"Is the Protestant pastor there?"

"Yes."

"Bring him out. We have looked into his case and find that he was arrested on a false accusation. He did not have a transmitter, only a radio, so the colonel has ordered that he be released. Bring him out."

So at two o'clock they brought me out, and I sat with the Simbas — and rested. At six o'clock a car came for me and took me to the mission, after the necessary release papers had been signed.

At the mission I found the brethren watching the road and waiting for me, just as they had when Peter was arrested and put in Herod's prison. Then, too, the church prayed faithfully that God would release him. And I remembered how God sent an angel to release Peter from prison because of the prayers of the church.

I rejoice because God heard the prayers of my church for me, and released me, too, from prison.

Please pray for my children, who were scattered when the Simbas came. I have heard nothing from them. Please pray for them, that God will keep them even as He kept me, for our lives are in His hands. The Bible says, "If we live, we live to God; if we die, we die to God."

Before I had been arrested, I was afraid. But after I was arrested, all fear left me and I considered death as nothing. Even when they told us we were being taken to be executed, it seemed as nothing.

Wasolo hospital staff, including two short-term medical helpers. Dr. Carlson worships with Congolese (right). *(Smith Kline & French)*

Congolese, whose arm was cut off by Rebels, is led away by friends. *(UPI)*

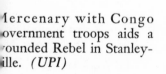

Mercenary with Congo government troops aids a wounded Rebel in Stanley-ville. *(UPI)*

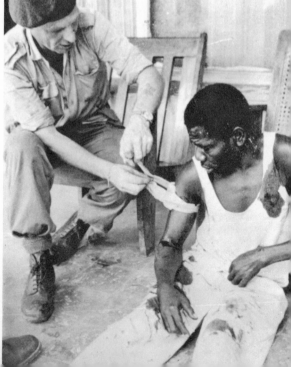

8/Modern Moses

At Oicha, in the northern part of the Congo, was a large medical work of the Africa Inland Mission. Before the revolt, Dr. Carl Becker and a dedicated staff of missionaries and Africans cared for an average of two thousand patients each day.

When the Rebels approached Oicha, Dr. Becker and the other missionaries were forced to evacuate this important facility. The African staff continued at the hospital, believing that they would be safe. Surely the Rebels would recognize the strategic importance of their medical work, and would not interfere.

They were wrong. The Rebels who murdered the only Congolese national medical doctor on the streets of Stanleyville — simply because he was educated — had no higher opinion of the mission hospital.

Yonama Angondia, African director of the medical work at Oicha, tells what happened. In the quiet telling, his own heroism is revealed.

After the missionaries left the area, Rebels entered a village near the border between Irumu and Beni. There the National Army fought with them, and 400 Rebels were killed. The National soldiers carried these bodies to Oicha and Beni, where they threw them into the Semiliki River.

In two subsequent battles with the Rebels, the National Army was victorious. But then they left the area, and life became really difficult for us. Everyone in the villages carried arrows, spears or machetes, but these were no match for the Rebels' guns and other weapons.

With their heavy machinery, the Rebel army removed trees that had been cut down to block the roads. This happened during the night of September 22; when we heard about it the next morning, we began to prepare for evacuation.

The following night, at about two a.m., I gathered the nurses and other hospital workers, the pastors and some of the sick. They left by way of a stream which runs east of the hospital. We arranged to meet later at a hill about five kilometers away.

I remained alone at the hospital, checking on everything before I left. I also made final rounds of patients too sick to travel.

The next morning, National Army soldiers came to the hospital for medicine; they had walked all night. I gave them what they needed and told them to leave quickly. A short time later we heard much gunfire and many explosions, and we knew that a battle was being fought.

A few hours afterward, the strength of the National Army gave out, and the few soldiers who were left retreated in trucks.

"Get away from the road," they yelled at the people as they drove off. "Our strength is finished." So the people headed for the bush.

By early afternoon, the Rebels had come to the outskirts of the mission, on the Beni side. They had heavy weapons: 20 armored cars, machine guns and cannons. They circled the hospital. The patients were very fearful.

I went out in front of the hospital to see what was going on. There I could see that shells were being fired around the church building, from the Kano road (where I had recently gotten the people through), from the Beni road, and also across the valley toward our homes. One solid line of fire seemed to surround us, a line that was closing in toward the station.

Bullets were flying everywhere, and I could no longer stay in the front yard. The sick patients kept asking me what they should do.

I gathered everyone together in the hospital, told those who were too sick to travel to get down under the beds, and sent the rest out by a passage to the operating area.

When the Rebels started to enter the hospital, I ran out the west side.

I was now leading the sick who could walk, while the Rebels were shooting at us.

People from the leper colony called to me to come and hide in their houses quickly. The Rebels were shooting from the slopes of the stream (we were going through the stream-bed), and some people thought I had fallen.

"No, I haven't fallen yet," I told them.

Some of the sick people joined in with the lepers and said that I should hide in a house; but I said, "No, I won't enter a house, for they would just follow me there." The people followed me through the leper camp, and the Rebels were just a short distance behind, shooting at us constantly. This continued for about an hour, when we came to the Oicha river.

I followed the river so that their gunfire was going over my head. The sick people who followed me were very frightened, but not one was wounded. We went right through the river and up the opposite bank.

When we got on the far bank, the Rebels could see us again, and began shooting. "Fall to the ground!" I called. "Walk on your knees, and put leaves and shrubbery on your head." So we began to move like snakes on the ground.

In this way we continued to go through the bush, while they shot over our heads. When I decided to cross over to the other side, I told those who were too weak to go any farther that they should just lie there. The rest should continue to follow me.

I told the weak ones, who would be staying, that we would shake the grass over our heads so that the Rebels would follow us with their gunfire, but they would only be hitting the grass.

We again followed the Oicha river, walking now through the tall grass. They continued to follow us for two hours, shooting at us. But God spared all our lives.

When we came to the place where the Oicha and Asefu rivers meet, I went between the two rivers. We walked from two o'clock in the afternoon until six o'clock, when we finally came to a hunter's camp. There we waited overnight.

The next morning I sent someone back to the mission station to see what damage had been done. On his return, the man reported that seven people had been killed. One of these was Gidiona, a teacher who had become a shop owner. The Rebels thought I was in the doctor's office, at his house, so they broke all the windows there. They searched for Dr. Becker, wanting to kill him first. Since they couldn't find him, they tried to find me, to kill me in his place.

At this time, the Rebels sent me this word: "Yonama, we

saw you when you escaped. Although we shot at you, the shots would not hit you. Because of this, we wanted you to stay here so you could show us the workings of the hospital, but you did wrong by escaping. Therefore you should return, because we won't leave unless we see you first."

I then sent another man back to find out how and why the people had been killed. He returned and told me that the Rebels had cut open the skulls of some so that they could remove their brains. Pieces of flesh had been cut from others, and then they had been sewed up. They put guards over the mission and hospital, so no one could disrupt anything.

At eleven o'clock that morning, planes flew over and dropped 16 bombs. At this time I told those who had followed me this far that I was going to move on, but that they should stay where they were.

I and one other man continued through the Ituri forest, following near the Ituri river. All day long we traveled in the underbrush, through mud and swamps. In the evening we came close to the main road. I was now headed for the place where I had left the original group of people, to the east of the hospital.

At seven o'clock the next morning, I came to my garden behind the main road, and there I talked with those who were guarding it. An hour later I left them, and went on to my home. Next I left the Oicha road and made my way east. I walked all through the day and night, with rain beating down the whole time, because I didn't want anyone from Oicha to know where I was going. I walked until I came to the hill, where I met the others whom I had sent there the night trouble began. This was at seven o'clock in the morning.

All the pastors, nurses, Christians, children and wives gathered around me quickly, and I told them how God had led me from Oicha, and how He had brought us together again.

They had received word that I was cut up with a knife, so I assured them that God had surely saved my life. I told them that it was only by God's power that we had come together again.

Now I said, "The time has come for us to start moving. We can't stay here, because they will come and kill us all. So we must cross the Semiliki."

I went ahead of the group, and kept a little way ahead of the rest, in case there were any enemies along the way.

As we left the hill, eleven soldiers of the National Army, who had been in the battle before, came up to me. "We are thankful that you are alive," they said, "but you must not leave because we may have to call on you. You must not leave here because the planes will be back to drop bombs."

"I am just going to this village to get some food," I said. I did not let them know that I planned to cross the border.

As we came to another road, we entered Poto, an unfriendly village. The people there said, "You must not go on, because Dr. Becker put you in charge as director, to help us with operations, maternity and other medicines. If you go, we will all die. You cannot go."

The chief called all the people of that village together. The big men all had arrows, spears or machetes, and the chief had a gun. He said I should tell them where I was going. They wouldn't let me leave, but said they would make me a home in the bush. They gave us a place to sleep, so I went to get all my people settled in.

One of the Christians in that village called me aside. "These people are saying that you shouldn't go on because they want to give you over to the enemy, the Rebels. Some say they will leave you in the bush. Others say they will kill you. Be very careful in talking to them."

I therefore gathered my thoughts quickly, while I was getting the people settled down.

As I returned to the village group, they were talking in their language, Kindoba. They said to me, "Now tell us truthfully what is on your mind."

"We have a dispensary across the valley, at Luanoli," I said, "so I and the pastors and nurses want to take our wives, children and young girl nurses to stay there. Once we have gotten our families there, we nurses will return to do the work at Oicha. At the moment things are bad at Oicha, because planes are coming in with bombs. The work cannot continue as usual. We want to wait a bit to see if things get better."

They objected, "That won't do, because the people and nurses at Luanoli won't help us. The Talingas are difficult people and they won't let us go over there. Our hospital is Oicha, so you will stay here with us. We will make a house for you in the tall grass, so the Rebels won't find you. We will guard you carefully."

"You have reasoned this out well," I replied. "For myself, I could agree, but for the hungry children it just won't do. Now I will have to lead the children over there, then I will return to see the place you have prepared for me so I can stay here and wait."

"All right," they said. "If you want to listen to those people there, and you don't want to listen to us, you'll have to pay us fifteen thousand francs before we'll let you go. But you must return."

"Good," I agreed. "But I left all the francs at Oicha. This whole thing caught me in the midst of my work, and I didn't have any time to think of francs. I have a few francs in my pocket; but if you want, go ahead and lead my people to safety and I will give you these few francs. Then you can take me and hand me over to the Rebels like you want to. The Rebels have already shot at me for two hours and couldn't hit me.

"Now I want to tell you something!

"For twenty years I have stayed among you. I have helped Dr. Becker with your children, your wives and many of your people, so you have been helped over and over again. Just this week I helped one of your men with a strangulated hernia and he is still alive today. Therefore, if you are not thankful for all that I have done for you, go ahead and turn me over to the enemy. But you must lead these wives, nurses, pastors and children to safety. I don't know if God will deliver me from your hands."

When they heard this, they began to melt. They said, "All right, because of all you have done for us these many years, we will only charge you three thousand francs."

"Fine," I said. "I have three thousand francs here." And I gave the francs to them. [Equivalent: eight dollars.]

"Now you may go," they said, "with all the nurses, wives, children and nursing students. You may go on over, and you must make a good hospital and dispensary there. If possible, you will open the way so that we and our people can come to you for medicine.

"However, because Pastor Zefania is a Nandi, he and the other Nandis must stay with us, together with those who are from the Mbuba tribe. The chief of the Talingas across the border would do them harm. But all you others can go ahead."

We were then free to go, but before leaving we had a Christian meeting with them. I prayed much that many would accept Christ, and that they would cling to that faith and follow God.

There was one man with us from Sumaline. Now they started talking about him. "You can go with all your people," they said, "but why did you bring this different colored man with you? Maybe you should return him to the Rebels so that they can kill him or wound him."

I said, "This man came with us because he was at the hospital. I gave him a bed because he was very sick. He is from the *Societe du Ituri*, and he usually transports palm fat for us there. Now if someone is sick, I do not choose them for color; I try to help every one. This man was on his way back to Beni, but the battle hindered his return and caused him to flee with us. We have been together in the bush, and God has entrusted his life to my hands. So if you want to fight with this man, you are fighting with the sick in general. You should, therefore, give this man the opportunity of going with us."

The chief gave his decision. "Yonama paid for all the hospital people, and he has done well to give us the three thousand francs. If he wants it, we should let the man go along with him right now."

They immediately started to say good-by to us so we could leave. I quickly sent a Christian to tell all our people to get ready, and had one of the nurses see that everyone was there and ready to go.

I followed the road above the Semiliki, walking with the fellow from Sumaline. After we had gone about ten kilometers, a friend of mine from Oicha caught up with us. He was riding a bike.

"They are searching diligently for you. They know you are going to Uganda, so you must hurry on." He gave me his bike and told me to hurry ahead.

I rode on to the Semiliki. There I met fishermen, among whom I found several friends. "The nurses are following," I told them, "so if they come to you here at night, you should give them a place to sleep."

"We will guard them," they promised.

I told them that I was planning to cross over to the dispensary at Luanoli. They said that we couldn't cross the Semiliki because the chief on the other side had put up a big barrier and was guarding it closely with men who had arrows, spears and machetes. If I tried to cross over, they said, these men would kill me.

"Don't worry about me," I told them. "The way will open up before me."

When the people following me came to this place, they were very frightened by the news of this trouble across the Semiliki. They thought they couldn't cross. They also heard rumors that fishermen had killed the man with me, that they had cut off his head and thrown it into the water.

In spite of all this, God helped me to open the way quickly for all our people. When I arrived on the other side, I found that the chief had actually put armed men on guard. But when I saw the men, I recognized many who had been to Oicha for treatment. Others had actually worked in my garden. So when they saw me, their faces lighted up. No one had ever come over to them to give them the Gospel, because everyone was afraid of the area. So I found that I was among friends. They said, "Greetings! Open the barrier quickly."

When I was on the other side, I said, "Will you give me a place to sit down, as I am very tired?"

"Bring a chair quickly!" they shouted.

So we conversed for a while, and I told them about the battles that had taken place. I also said to them, "You rebels, who told you to put up this barrier and stand guard like this?"

"Chief Baskari."

"He has put you in a position of sure death," I told them. "The Rebels don't like barriers, or spears, or arrows, or machetes. If they find people doing this, they will kill the whole village. You have set yourselves up to be killed."

At this they began to be frightened.

We continued to talk for a while. Then they said, "You write a letter to Chief Baskari. Because you are tired, he will come to get you. You should tell him all you have told us, because he has put us in this dangerous position."

The people there gave us fish and started to prepare other food for us. They took care of the bike I had been traveling on. I began to eat.

The chief came quickly, and as soon as I finished eating, he said, "Now tell me all about this."

I told him about the situation, and then I suggested that he should accompany me across the border with all those who held any position in the government; because the Rebels didn't like anyone who was connected with the government. I told him that the Rebels had been killing those in authority, the police and soldiers. Therefore, those holding bows and arrows would be killed with the other villagers.

This scared the chief and everyone in the area so that they took down the barrier and threw the pieces far away. They knew it wouldn't be safe behind a barrier.

I told the chief about those who were coming behind me, and explained that there were about 200 of them. I asked him to instruct the villagers to let them pass through unharmed — because we were going on ahead. The chief agreed.

The chief stayed there for a time, and gave me his truck to take me to his camp. So we piled in some women, children and things to go to the chief's "city."

When we arrived, I left all the people at the chief's place, Kamango, while I went to stay with the African pastor. I told the pastor that there were pastors and people coming behind, and suggested that he go along with us across to Uganda. "But right now," I told him, "I am going to Luanoli to close up the medical work and pack up the medicines, and to talk with the medical committee there."

The next morning another friend of mine came on a bike to tell me to hurry on my way. So I started off to Luanoli and told the pastor to continue on toward Uganda when my people arrived.

When I came to the dispensary, I called all the sick people together and gave them the news. Then I told them all to hold on to their medical cards, because the Rebels had destroyed all the records at Oicha. I talked with the church people along with the elders and the medical committee, saying, "I am closing the dispensary here along with all the medicines. I haven't decided whether we will take them to Uganda or hide them here."

So we worked at packing the medicines.

Soon my friend on the bicycle came again and said, "The Rebels are only seven kilometers behind you. You told me the nurses would pack the medicines and you would go on across to Uganda. Why are you waiting here?"

Therefore, my friend and the Christians of that place would not let me go back to the regular road to Uganda. Instead they took me up to Mount Ruwenzori. Part of the time they pushed me on the bike, because by this time my strength was finished. The chief's men and the Christians pushed me until we came right to the Uganda border.

At that point I said "good-by" to Congo and crossed the river that runs along the border. All the rest of my people had preceded me, and were together at Bundibugio.

All the Christians, the hospital staff, pastors, children — everyone, big and small — walked out of Oicha on foot, each carrying a small bag of some sort. On the long trip to Uganda, some got sores on their feet, others swelled up, and many others got sick. But God protected us all, and not one died on the way. Everyone who left Oicha came safely into Uganda.

After we crossed the Semiliki, word traveled fast back to

Oicha to the effect that Yonama had crossed over to Matalinga with the nurses. So the Rebels sent their men after us.

At the place where I paid three thousand francs to get through, the chief and his police, along with their leader, Mbema, ran into the bush to hide. They were found and were taken back to Oicha with their hands tied behind their backs. Two nurses, Suzana and Yakobede, who joined us later (they stayed behind at Oicha to help with some last minute cases), said they saw these eight men with their own eyes, and that the Rebels shot and killed them because they had let us go through their village.

Surely God gave us wisdom in dealing with them there; otherwise we would have been returned with them to Oicha to be killed.

Yonama led 195 people from Oicha to Uganda, not including many more who joined them along the way and came over to Uganda with them.

9/Writing

During September and October, 1964, the Simbas made many visits to Kilometer 8. They came to "inspect," which usually meant that they were looking for radio transmitters. One weekend Chuck counted ten separate inspections.

Times chosen for these visits were erratic: midnight, seven a.m., various times during the day. The visits were unsettling, and everyone was disturbed as the Simbas went through all the rooms, regardless of the hour.

When a car was heard on the road that went past the mission property, all the children were hurried into the house from the lawn where they were playing. The presence of anyone on the grounds was an encouragement to the Simbas to stop for yet another inspection.

They also stopped for food. This created a problem, since 75 meals had to be prepared each day from limited supplies, for those who lived at Kilometer 8. A senior missionary, such as Al Larson, usually undertook the delicate job of turning the Simbas away without the food they were seeking, yet without bad feelings.

One day a Simba came asking for food. "Give me meat," he demanded. "We have a pot of rice going down the road."

"Look," Al said, "we have 25 people here to feed every meal. You know that. You have rice! Now, how about giving me some rice for these 25 people?"

The Simba had never thought of that. So he apologized and went away — without any meat.

But such negotiations with the Simbas were never without danger. And everyone knew it.

The unspoken fears of the missionaries at Kilometer 8 were realized one Sunday afternoon at the beginning of November when two Simbas drove up in a car. Trucks had been passing on the road all morning.

"Everybody has to go with us into Stanleyville," they announced. "Now. Right away."

Bob McAllister, who was unusually skillful in dealing with the Congolese, asked if this was really necessary. Did everybody have to go, or just the men? And would there even be room for everybody to go — was transportation available?

The Simbas soon changed their minds. Only the men had to go. But all of them. Not just the Americans.

Ione McMillan tried to get Hector to pack a bag to take with him. But Hector smiled and refused. "If I take a bag along, they'll think I plan to stay. And I don't."

Steve Davis began to cry when he saw his father, with the other four men — Al Larson, Del Carper, Bob McAllister and Hector — get into the car.

"Don't cry, little boy," one Simba said. "Daddy's coming back." For once, a Lion was gentle.

Surprisingly, Steve stopped crying.

The men from Kilometer 8 were taken to Stanleyville's Hotel des Chutes by their Simba guards. There they were brought before Colonel Opepe, who made his headquarters in the hotel.

The colonel — distinguished by an unusually mild attitude toward missionaries — recognized Al Larson and Bob McAllister, who had conferred with him on previous occasions in connection with William Scholten's death in prison.

When Del Carper's hearing aid was discovered, the Simbas became excited. They thought it was a radio transmitter. (The Simbas seemed obsessed with fear that missionaries could keep in contact with the advancing mercenary army through transistor radios. Most of them seemed unable to distinguish between a transmitter and a receiver.)

Del was quickly silenced when he tried to explain that he could not hear well, and for that reason wore the hearing aid in his ear. After all, if he couldn't hear, he would certainly keep his ear open instead of sticking something in it that would plug it up!

While this discussion was going on, one Simba guard kept striking Chuck Davis on the side of his head, twisting his nose, and in other ways tormenting him — but always making sure that Colonel Opepe was not observing his actions.

To settle the matter, Colonel Opepe took the hearing aid into another room. His subordinates undertook to question the missionaries about their countries of origin. "Is Canada part of the United States?" they asked Hector McMillan. "What country is Brooklyn?" they asked Chuck Davis.

The colonel came out. He was satisfied about the hearing aid and returned it to Del. But a short time later, the instrument was confiscated again, this time for good.

"Throw them in that room!" he ordered. And the missionaries joined other prisoners in a small hotel room. For the next three weeks, four men slept on the two single beds, while three more slept on the floor.

As soon as the car had disappeared on the road to Stanley-ville, the nine women who were left behind had a prayer meeting. They were well aware of their own vulnerable position, increased by the presence of 14 children. So they asked the Lord, if it was His will, to make it possible for them to stay at Kilometer 8, and to protect them there.

Having prayed, the women returned to their work.

When a German missionary, Volker Gscheidle, came out from Stanleyville the next day to stay with them, the women were sure that God had answered their prayer. He remained until Hector McMillan and Bob McAllister, Canadian and British, returned a week later, when they were released through the efforts of the British consul.

Congolese Christians who lived and worked on the mission property found it hard to understand how the missionary wives could go about their normal activities — even smile occasionally — when their husbands were imprisoned in Stanley-ville.

Why weren't they sad? Sad like the Congolese, for instance. They cried a lot during these troubled times, and were thoroughly upset.

The difference in their attitude was difficult for the women to explain to the Africans.

They didn't really try to explain. They were too busy maintaining a normal atmosphere for their children. They knew, as mothers, that their attitude toward the depressing, dangerous situation would set the pattern for the children's response — and have not only immediate, but long-range results.

Besides, they really trusted God. "We weren't play-acting," Muriel Davis explains. They trusted Him for their husbands, for their children, for themselves.

Four times each day everyone stopped work for prayer meetings: at eight and ten o'clock in the morning, four in the afternoon, and nine at night. But those were the group meetings for prayer. "Actually," Muriel says, "we were praying all the time."

At first the women and children prayed together. Later, when a crisis seemed to be approaching, separate prayer meetings were held for the adults and the children.

Under house arrest, concerned for their husbands imprisoned in Stanleyville's Hotel des Chutes, subject to constant harassment from gun-toting Simbas . . . the women were planning Saturday night supper.

"Let's have something special."

"How about hamburgers again? I can make rolls as easily as bread from the dough that's rising. (Bread-making was Muriel Davis' special job.)

"Don't you think the kids are getting a little tired of those corned-beef patties we call hamburgers? It would be nice if we could have something different."

"Guess what I found yesterday, when I was cleaning out the pantry: some canned hot dogs. Don't ask me where I got them in the first place — I don't remember. But we can really have a feast tonight if we use them."

"Do you have enough?"

"I think so. But maybe you should make corned-beef patties for the grownups."

"I wonder what the fellows are getting to eat in Stan." Muriel looked up from the dough she was kneading.

"As long as they're still eating, it doesn't much matter, does it?" Ione McMillan spoke gently.

"No, it doesn't. And for that matter, I find it harder and harder doing these special things out here. I mean, when you know what's going on, and what could happen at any moment."

"But we're doing them for the children. We have to try to keep their morale up. So anything we can do to make life seem normal to them is worth the trouble."

"I know that, Ione. And I'm so thankful for what your kindergarten is meaning to Steve. He loves it. And he's learning so much. For awhile I was so worried about what the past couple of months would do to him and little Beth emotionally."

Gray-haired, practical Ione McMillan — mother of six sons — walked across the room and put her hand on the younger woman's shoulder. "My dear, the Lord has promised that He'll take care of whatever we've committed to Him. We've all committed our children, haven't we?"

"Yes, and He *has* been taking care of them. I can't doubt it since that night when I said good-by to Chuck at the airport, and the Lions pushed us into the automobile."

"Speaking of the children, does anyone know what Hector's been doing with the older ones this morning?"

Ione McMillan's eyes brightened, and she smiled. "I couldn't guess. All I know is that he was saying something at breakfast about how one bathroom wasn't enough for all these people, and he was going to do something about it."

"If anyone can improve the situation, it's Hector. Do you remember last Saturday and the broken washing machine?"

The women laughed.

"Those older boys will do anything for him. He had them working all morning hitching the machine to the engine that grinds the wheat. When they finally got that job done, it was noon, and they hadn't even started the wash. But after lunch they all pitched in and worked all afternoon doing the wash."

"And not a complaint, either."

"Hector really knows how to handle them."

"I think his secret is his patience, and his imagination. He even makes dishwashing exciting to the kids."

"Yes, I was watching his crew work last night. Hector placed Marilyn here, John over there, and one other child — I forget who it was — over there. Then they went to work, after he'd explained his new system. It was fun to watch."

"And they finished the dishes in half the time it takes the other crews."

"Ione, is it true that Hector won't pack a bag with things for an emergency departure, like the rest of us have?"

"It is. He absolutely refuses. I've asked him time and again. He did finally agree to pack some of the children's things, and stow them away up in the rafters in case we had to leave in a hurry. But not for himself."

"I don't know what we'd do without him."

"Let's go see what project he has the children involved in this time. You said something about another bathroom, Ione. We could certainly use one."

They found Hector outside the Hangar, tapping the water tank. The younger children were carrying roofing tiles from a little distance away, while the older boys were using the tiles to construct a cubicle.

"We were just talking about you, Hector, and decided to find out what you're doing this time."

"Can you guess?" Hector turned toward them from the tank.

"Ione gave us a hint. She said you were talking about doing something about the crowded conditions in the bathroom."

"And I am. You see a new shower for Kilometer 8. Now everyone can have a bath each day without waiting in line. Even the kids."

10/The Beloved Hector

HECTOR MCMILLAN was a Scotch Canadian, raised on a farm in Stormont County, Ontario. Although his parents always had family worship, Hector grew up without coming to grips with Jesus Christ personally.

When he was 21 years of age, his cousin — E. R. Thompson, of the West Indies Mission — visited in the McMillan home. "Why don't you go to Prairie Bible Institute?" the missionary asked. So Hector went. Mr. Thompson and other relatives were praying that Hector would find Christ — and he did, the very first week of school.

Then, and in later life, Hector resented all the years he had spent in church without ever being given a clear invitation to receive Christ.

At Moody Bible Institute, meanwhile, Ione Reed was a student. When John and Betty Stam were martyred in China by the Communists, Ione offered her life to God as a missionary. After graduation, she went to Toronto as a candidate of the Unevangelized Fields Mission.

Hector was in the Royal Canadian Air Force when he first met Ione. He had already sensed God's call to missionary service, and applied for an early discharge so that he could go to the field.

By the time the red tape of his release had unwound, Ione was already in the Congo. Hector proceeded to qualify as a candidate of the same mission under which Ione was serving, and also told Ione's mother — who was a widow — that he was interested in marrying her daughter. With her approval, he then wrote a proposal of marriage to the young Congo missionary. A minister friend helped him compose the letter. Ione responded with a brief cable: "Ruth 1:16" (". . . whither thou goest, I will go; and where thou lodgest, I will lodge: thy people shall be my people, and thy God my God").

But there were to be delays. Ione finished an initial term of three years in the Congo before she returned home for her furlough — and Hector.

When the ship docked in New York, Ione told the American vice-consul of Angola, with whom she'd become acquainted, "You'll recognize Hector: he's bald, and he'll be carrying a box of candy under his arm."

The vice-consul was cleared through customs before Ione, and at the pier he did recognize Hector from Ione's description.

"Listen, fellow," he said, "if you're Hector McMillan, you'd better hurry and get a box of candy."

During Ione's furlough, the couple planned to be married. But when the way suddenly opened up for Hector to go out to the Congo, he seized the opportunity and postponed the wedding.

After Ione returned from her furlough, they were married in the Congo. The service was simple, and Chester and Dolena Burk stood up with Hector and Ione. (Years later, Chester would die in the same Congo bloodbath with Hector.)

The following meditation on his life as a missionary was written by Hector a few years after he went to the Congo:

"The Lord will never cease to help us until we cease to need it."

I find it difficult to stay in that place of realizing that I need His help. Self-sufficiency would make us independent. The mission field is a good cure for such a person. During the past year I have frequently found myself in tight corners.

It is so easy for confusion and frustration to displace an ordered life, but God is not the Author of confusion.

One day, in the carpenter shop, things were not going very well. Each of the Congolese carpenters was doing a different job, and they all had to be watched lest they should waste materials and time. Just when things were at their worst, a small group of schoolboys came for their class.

I went into an adjoining room, knelt down, and quieted my heart in prayer. The trouble was not in my surroundings but within me.

Adaptability is one of the first qualifications of a missionary. One must learn to be all things to all men. Even the best of training in the homeland seems inadequate. When we get into difficulties, we naturally long for more talents to cope with them effectively. But this verse from the Psalmist comes to mind: "Thou hast enlarged me when I was in distress." Each new experience pushes back our horizon.

Buildings must be erected. At home we call in a contractor. He engages an architect. Then stonemasons, bricklayers, carpenters, plumbers, electricians, interior decorators and painters all have their part in the work.

But in the Congo, the missionary is the amalgamation of all

these specialists. If the building has any faults or defects, he has no one to blame but himself.

It would be very distressing indeed if we could not inquire at the footstool of the great Master Builder. Dependence on Him dissolves our difficulties. He gives us wisdom to utilize our meager knowledge. When we do not know, He simply guides.

One experience I cannot forget. I went into the government post one day to get the weekly mail. While waiting for the truck to come from Stanleyville, I was sitting on the porch of a building listening to the big tribal chief decide matters as they were brought to him. Presently some Congolese policemen, in their important red hats, herded a group of eight men up to the chief. They were a shabby, dejected lot and the chief looked them over. Their crime was that of stealing money and clothing from a nearby store.

When all had given witness, the judgment was given. Vainly they protested; justice must hold sway. Three men were convicted. They were chained together and led to the prison.

This whole matter weighed heavily on me, so I wandered down that way and asked the guard if I could go in. He said I could, so I entered the prison. There these three men sat in their gloom and misery. What better opportunity could one wish for?

It was evident that they needed someone to free them from physical bondage, but that was not within my power. But there was another binding power that was even stronger. I was thankful that they were willing to listen while I told of the wages of sin. Their faces showed that they were hardened sinners, but Christ Jesus came into the world to save sinners. As best I could, I tried to make plain God's way of deliverance, seeking to turn them from darkness to light, and from the power of Satan to God.

The saying that a watched pot never boils can be applied to missionary work. We are so close to it all the time, always observing the lives of our people, that when various ones are transformed we are scarcely aware of it. They are, however, growing in grace, casting off heathen customs, and witnessing for the Lord.

The McMillans spent 23 years in the Congo, mostly at Bongondza. They had six sons. Their last years, immensely happy ones, were spent at Kilometer 8, the station five miles from Stanleyville. From 1955 to 1960, Hector and Ione were responsible for 26 children of U.F.M. couples. After Congo's independence in 1960, the local school, which the children attended, deteriorated to such an extent that another provision was necessary. And so the McMillans gave up their charges, along with their own children of school age, and all the children were enrolled as boarding students at the Africa Inland Mission school at Rethi.

The authorities of the school at Rethi asked Hector and Ione to come as houseparents, and there is little doubt that the invitation was an attractive one. They loved children, and they could continue to raise their own children in their own home.

But the McMillans gave no immediate answer. Instead, as was their settled conviction, they turned the request over to the field council for its decision. The council — which now included Africans — considered the matter, then denied the request. They wanted Hector and Ione to stay at the bush station, Kilometer 8.

That decision, accepted by the McMillans as those who were under authority, determined their presence at the station a few years later. In that crisis, such a couple — loving, secure, wise, sensible — was desperately needed by the little band of missionary women and children who found refuge at Kilometer 8.

As a father responsible for six sons, Hector McMillan didn't just pray, "Dear Lord, bless Ken." Instead, he claimed a Bible verse for Ken *each day*, and one for each of the other five. Then he prayed that God would make this particular verse true in the life of his son. He never claimed the same verse twice. In a tiny script he wrote the verses, or enough to give the thought — more than six thousand of them — in his notebook.

Eventually the plan was such a blessing to Hector that he began to share the verses with the boys. Ken, the oldest, remembers one verse in particular that his father sent to him while he was away at school: "Be not conformed to this world" (Romans 12:2). Hector was particularly fond of the Psalms; as a result, many verses came from that part of the Bible.

All the boys were away from home, at school, for the two years immediately before the final Congo incidents. When the crisis came, they — together with the other children at Rethi — were sent home to be with their parents.

The McMillan boys have happy memories of family worship, especially during the final months at Kilometer 8. Each morning their parents woke them early enough for each boy to have his own personal time of Bible reading. Then later, before breakfast, their mother and father came into the boys' room for family reading. (Kilometer 8 was so crowded that the McMillans only had two rooms.)

Hector began these family times by sharing a chapter, or part of a chapter, on a book he himself was reading. The life of Hudson Taylor (who founded the China Inland Mission, now the Overseas Missionary Fellowship); books by A. W. Tozer (especially his *Knowledge of the Holy*); V. Raymond Edman's *Disciplines*; and a history of the Reformation: these are especially remembered by the older McMillan boys because their father read them aloud in family worship during the months before he was killed.

But the Bible was something special. "Each day Dad read the Bible at the very end, in our family worship," Ken recalls. "He kept the best for last."

Even in his Bible reading, Hector took a creative approach. This, coupled with the unfeigned godliness of their parents, was doubtless the reason family worship was the highlight of the day for the McMillan boys. The reading followed a recurring schedule. Monday was the day for reading from the Pentateuch; Hector simply began where he had left off the previous Monday. Tuesday was for another section of the Bible, with a week between readings. So with Wednesday and the other days: each involved reading from a special part of the Bible.

Bible drills (to develop speed in locating references, but also to familiarize the boys with the Bible) and memorization contributed still more variety. Unlike many Christian homes, family worship at the McMillans' was never dull.

Chuck Davis says, "I'm sort of ashamed to admit it, but while I was staying at Kilometer 8, I sometimes stood outside the door of the McMillan boys' room while Hector was leading family worship, just to listen. It was fascinating, and spiritually moving."

This attitude toward the Bible, and toward family worship, didn't suddenly develop in crisis days.

When the children were small, Hector cut out a piece of cardboard for each child, with his name on it. The child was expected to sit still on his personal "place mat" on the floor, during Bible reading, and with his eyes closed during prayer. When the children grew older, each had a stool.

The children could be noisy at other times — family worship was a time for reverence.

Ione recalls that all this meant discipline for her, too. "Breakfast had to be ready before we started family worship. I tried

HECTOR AND IONE MCMILLAN with six sons: (from left) Timothy (8), Kenneth (15), David (12), Stephen (9), Paul (14), John (10). Below are Mrs. McMillan and her sons after their return to the United States.

to keep it quite simple, but even so, I had to get up at 4:30 in the morning to get it ready.

"If you really want to honor the Lord in family worship," Ione concludes, "you'll find the way."

But this only gives one side of Hector. There were many others.

He had, in Ione's words, "a cackling laugh." His stories were famous among the missionaries.

When the McMillans returned from their last furlough, Hector could hardly wait to tell some new ones he had picked up in the States. That particular trip back, they took a Chevrolet truck with them, and Hector accompanied it on a ship (to save money on shipping costs). Ione returned by plane.

As a result, Ione arrived at the Kilometer 8 station several days before her husband. When Hector finally drove up in the truck, he told a funny story to the missionaries who welcomed him.

"Oh, Ione already told us that," they said. Hector was crestfallen, and his gloom deepened over the next few days at finding that Ione had told all his stories before he arrived.

But Hector was an optimist who soon was laughing at the way his wife had gotten one up on him.

The two-ton truck turned out to be a major help to the mission. Hector (whose most obvious ability was along mechanical and building lines) added an extra gas tank, installed a box on one side to carry food on trips, and another box to carry tools. He also made frames for handling a load of wood on the truck, and a top and benches for carrying children to school.

Hector McMillan was a "missionaries' missionary." His spirit, his home, his work lessened the burdens of other missionaries. And the others were associated with various missionary societies.

He once said, "I consider it a privilege to be a servant to the servants of Jesus Christ." Commenting on this statement, Al Larson, leader of the Unevangelized Fields Mission forces that went through the Congo uprising, says: "More than anyone else, Hector put himself out to meet the physical needs of the Congolese and his fellow missionaries. His happy spirit and rich laughter always lifted us up when we tended to be discouraged."

Here was a man of God, and he was ideally paired with Ione. Even if she sometimes spoiled his jokes.

Hector McMillan and Bob McAllister, citizens of Canada and Great Britain, were detained at the Hotel des Chutes for a week. Then the British consul arranged for their release.

"During that week," Charles Davis says, "I saw something happen to Hector's face. A sort of glow came over it, something I can't explain. But it was there. You could see it, and it made a great impression on me.

"Hector never once prayed for his own deliverance, not just then, but during all those months. Some of us were weaker — we did pray that God would bring us out of all that mess. But Hector never prayed that way. He prayed for the deliverance of his family, of his wife and his boys, but never once for himself."

When Hector returned to Kilometer 8, he did something he had never done in all his previous years of marriage. He began to hand responsibility for his sons over to his wife, Ione. And he spoke with Ione about the unimportance of a person's body. The important thing, he said, is that a Christian who dies is with Christ right away — his body isn't really important.

"Somehow I got the feeling," Chuck says, "that both Hector McMillan and Paul Carlson — whom I got to know later — knew that soon they would be with their Lord."

11/Three Martyrs

DAVID LIVINGSTONE, in the infancy of missions in the Congo, gave his "Estimate of the kind of Men needed in Africa":

"Missionaries ought to be men of high moral and intellectual attainment, of tried and undoubted godliness. They ought to be men with the capacity to exert commanding influence if they remained in their own native country.

"Missionaries need mental energy to look into all the windings and intricacies of character, habits, feelings and motives of men who do not have the Father's love in their hearts.

"They must be big enough men to acquire the art of influencing heathen minds; to reduce unwritten and strange languages to understandable forms; to call into exercise energies that have slumbered for centuries.

"We need men who will endure patiently the reverses, trials and disappointments which inevitably accompany missionary life.

"This requires the best and ablest men the Church can furnish."

The Congo martyrs were such men and women.

Chester Burk was a farmer, his wife, Dolena, a school teacher. They had a farm in Sundre, Alberta. For some time they had felt a call to missionary work, but had put off any serious consideration of the matter. For one thing, Chester was "hesitant and fearful about the Bible school training necessary."

Their farm was prospering and they were busy. "I tried to make myself believe that this was God's place for me, but God's Spirit gave me no rest."

One wintry day, in a field of crusted snow, Chester was confronted by a wild boar, which was foaming at the mouth. Chester used a stick to repel the vicious animal, until it broke in his hand. Then he fled from what seemed to be certain death. His escape across the snow was slowed by the crust that broke under his weight.

But he got to a haystack, which he hurriedly climbed. On this uncertain perch, looking down at the wild animal, Chester gave in: "All right, Lord, I'll go to Bible school."

"It was then," Chester wrote, "that the full force of I Corinthians 6:19 and 20 came to my heart: 'What? know ye not that your body is the temple of the Holy Ghost which is in you, which ye have of God, and ye are not your own? For ye are bought with a price: therefore glorify God in your body, and in your spirit, which are God's.' I put my hand to the plow — not to look back."

As soon as he could get the affairs of the farm settled, Chester went to Prairie Bible Institute. There his mind was settled on Africa, in which he had been interested as long as he could remember.

After completion of the course, Chester and Dolena went to the Congo as missionaries of the Unevangelized Fields Mission. There he served as an evangelist, builder and Bible teacher.

Chester was an outdoorsman. He often hunted for the food needs of the Congolese, killing game — sometimes an elephant — and giving it to them for meat. This identification with the country and people of the Congo, together with his farm background, probably explains Chester's unusual ability to communicate Bible truths to the Congolese. He used many illustrations from farming and outdoor life in his preaching and teaching.

Here is an account, in Chester's own words, of an incident in his missionary life in the Congo, some years before independence:

The worst heat of the day was over, so we strolled through the sleepy village to invite the people to the evening service. Some came out eagerly to meet us, grasping our hands in both of theirs, while others called their greetings from their doorways. Children sometimes ventured up to us, with grimy hands outstretched. The more timid ran screaming from us to their mothers, who seemed to take a special delight in dragging their kicking, yelling youngsters to us to make them shake hands. The more they kicked and screamed, the greater was the amusement of the villagers.

Two men were sitting in the shade of a tree making arrows, and we stopped to talk. Chairs were promptly brought out and we sat with them for some time. One, the headman of the village, had recently been discharged from the Congo military forces. He had seen plenty of the white man's ways in the war, and we could see that he was not very favorably impressed.

A good crowd gathered at the evening service, and we noticed the old soldier among them. Again the next morning, he was present at the service, wearing a heavy army overcoat.

An invitation was given at the close for anyone who wanted to accept Christ as Saviour. One woman with a baby in her arms responded; that was all. She was asked to come up to the rest-house, away from the crowd, where we would pray with her. Nearly half the crowd followed us, however, while the rest dispersed.

As we went, I looked back and saw the old soldier still sitting in his chair as he had during the service. He was staring at the ground in front of him, apparently absorbed in thought.

At the rest-house we found that there were four, including the mother, who wished to accept Christ as Saviour. While we were dealing with them, this old man also came. I saw him standing there, as if he wished to speak with me, but I thought he only wanted to speak about porters to carry our camp outfit to the next village. So I paid no more attention to him.

What was my great surprise and joy, when my companion called out and said, "This man wants to accept Christ." On inquiry, I found that he did want to get rid of his burden of sin, and he — together with the other four — accepted Christ as Saviour, and confessed Him before the others.

In this village there is no resident evangelist, and we can only rarely visit. But we know that the little group of believers is in safe keeping, always in reach of the Master's hand.

At the time of Congo's independence in 1960, the Burks were subjected to threats, and even had guns poked into their stomachs. Then, just before their furlough, Chester had a serious illness. He went back to Canada a sick man.

But that last furlough was happy for the Burks. Chester went into the Peace River district of Alberta on a camping trip. There, in the foothills of the Rockies, he got lost on a sub-zero night. He built a fire at his feet, another at his head — and slept. The next day he found his way out.

In the uneasy political situation of the Congo, Chester wrote

Hector and Ione McMillan that he had a strange dread of returning to the country he loved after that furlough. But Chester and Dolena did return — "I put my hand to the plow — not to look back," as he had said years before.

Chester Burk was at Boyulu when the Rebels took over the whole Eastern Province. After much abuse and suffering, he was killed at the river in Bafwasende.

William McChesney was raised in a Free Methodist parsonage. People called him "Smiling Bill" because of his happy disposition. He lived in Phoenix, Arizona.

In 1960, Bill was in the final stage of preparation for the mission field at the headquarters of Worldwide Evangelization Crusade. Considering the life he was leaving, and what lay ahead, Bill wrote a poem called "My Choice" at this time:

> I want my breakfast served at eight,
> With ham and eggs upon the plate;
> A well-broiled steak I'll eat at one,
> And dine again when day is done.
>
> I want an ultra-modern home
> And in each room a telephone;
> Soft carpets, too, upon the floors,
> And pretty drapes to grace the doors.
>
> A cozy place of lovely things,
> Like easy chairs with inner springs,
> And then I'll get a small TV —
> Of course, "I'm careful what I see."

I want my wardrobe, too, to be
Of neatest, finest quality,
With latest style in suit and vest:
Why should not Christians have the best?

But then the Master I can hear
In no uncertain voice, so clear:
"I bid you come and follow Me,
The lowly Man of Galilee.

"Birds of the air have made their nest,
And foxes in their holes find rest,
But I can offer you no bed;
No place have I to lay My head."

In shame I hung my head and cried.
How could I spurn the Crucified?
Could I forget the way He went,
The sleepless nights in prayer He spent?

For forty days without a bite,
Alone He fasted day and night;
Despised, rejected — on He went,
And did not stop till veil He rent.

A Man of sorrows and of grief,
No earthly friend to bring relief;
"Smitten of God," the prophet said —
Mocked, beaten, bruised, His blood ran red.

If He be God, and died for me,
No sacrifice too great can be
For me, a mortal man, to make;
I'll do it all for Jesus' sake.

> Yes, I will tread the path He trod,
> No other way will please my God;
> So, henceforth, this my choice shall be,
> My choice for all eternity.

Bill McChesney went to the Congo a few days before that country's independence in 1960. There he served as a youth evangelist, visiting many different stations. Bill was also a good mechanic, and kept the mission trucks and cars going.

During November, 1964, Bill was taken prisoner, along with other WEC missionaries. His health at this time was quite poor. Jim Rodger, a young Scottish missionary, nursed Bill for the next two weeks.

The day after the Stanleyville massacre, Bill proved his earlier choice; like his Master, he was cruelly beaten, clubbed and speared, and finally thrown into the Wamba river.

Jim Rodger made a choice, too . . . like his Master. By declaring his British nationality, he would have been spared death with the Belgians and Americans. But he chose to stand with Bill to the end, and die.

12/More Congolese Heroes

JACQUES WAS AN EVANGELIST of Banjwadi-Ugwasi. The Rebels captured him and asked, "Why are you fighting against us?" (He was not actually fighting.)

"We are not fighting you," Jacques replied. "We are obeying God."

"Why are you fighting us?" Their voices were more angry as they repeated the question.

"Because we follow Christ. We're not with you because you refuse our Christ."

"Cut off his ear!" the leader shouted. And they did.

"Now, will you join us?"

"No, I'm a Christian."

"Make a fire." The leader waited until the fire was hot and there were coals.

"Now put his feet in it."

Jacques struggled in vain. His feet were held in the fire.

"Will you join us now?"

"Never," he moaned. "I follow Christ."

Seeing that physical pain alone was not enough to make the

evangelist change his mind, the leader held up a copy of the Bible.

"What does this book teach you?"

"About Christ."

"Does this book teach you that false prophets will come?"

"Yes, it does."

"So —" the leader shouted, "now you accuse us of being false prophets!"

"If you're not false prophets," Jacques asked, "why are you fighting Christ?"

At these words, they began to beat the evangelist with clubs. When he finally lost consciousness, they threw him aside, probably thinking he was dead.

When Jacques regained consciousness hours later, and found his captors gone, he slowly crawled to his village. There the Christians tenderly cared for him.

A certain pastor stood before the firing squad of Simba soldiers. He said that before they pulled the triggers of their rifles, he had one last request: "May I pray?"

Even the Simbas didn't refuse such a request. "Go ahead," the leader said.

"Lord, forgive these men," the pastor prayed. "They don't know what they are doing. But *You* know this Rebel movement, Father. If it is of You, if it can bring peace to the Congo, if it can help our land grow strong and beautiful, then prosper it and help these men to rule well. But Lord, You know all the blood they have shed, and all the bad they have done. Forgive them for all this. And if it is *not* Your will for them to rule, then *defeat* them."

Opening his eyes, expecting the shots to crash into his skull and body at the same moment, the pastor was surprised to find that he was alone. The Simba soldiers had melted away into the bush. They were unable to stand before the praying of this man of God.

On three other occasions, this pastor was present at large gatherings of the Congolese in his tribe when the Simbas brought them together for a political harangue. Each time, when the Simbas had finished their speeches, the pastor requested the right to speak. On receiving permission, he preached the Gospel to his own tribespeople and the Simbas, telling them that Jesus Christ is the only means of getting right with God.

On one other occasion he was arrested and severely beaten. Yet when he was released, he began to preach the Gospel again.

Mayambi Sosthene and his wife Pauline were students at the Banjwadi Theological school to which Charles and Muriel Davis came from America in April, 1964. At that time they were in their third year of study.

Mayambi was 28 years of age, the son of Christian parents. He was a Mennonite, with 12 years' training at the mission school in Nyanga. During his schooling, Mayambi trusted Christ and became a member of the church. In 1958 he completed the teacher training course; the same year he married Koloma Pauline, a Nyanga girl.

After several years of teaching at other villages, Mayambi was called back to Nyanga, as director of the school from which he himself had been graduated.

When the Banjwadi school was about to open, late in 1961, Mayambi told the annual Mennonite church conference that he felt God was leading him to undertake further training for His work.

And so he and Pauline were in the first class to enter the Banjwadi Theological school. They enjoyed their studies, and Mayambi's experience was recognized. He was asked to represent the local church at the annual meeting of the Congo Protestant Council.

In January, 1964 — three months before the Davis family arrived at Banjwadi — Mayambi had his first hint of Rebel trouble. It was on a trip to eastern and southern Congo that he heard reports of Rebel activities.

By this time Pauline had given birth to two sons, Basil and Emmanuel. Another couple from Nyanga had also come to the seminary, Bahatuila Jean and his wife Mutena.

The course at Banjwadi was four years in length. Mayambi considered returning home at the end of the third year, but decided to stay on despite rumors of Rebel trouble.

That summer Mayambi did Christian work in the villages that surround Stanleyville. Thus he and Pauline were there when the Rebels took over the city in August. (It was at this time that Charles and Muriel Davis were first taken captive.)

Most of the missionaries at Banjwadi had either left, or were under arrest elsewhere. September and October were uneasy, fearful months for the few who remained, as well as for Mayambi and the other Congolese who continued at the station.

One day in October, Rebels made one of their frequent appearances at Banjwadi, and this time ordered all the foreign missionaries to pack their suitcases. Mayambi sided with the missionaries, helping them, and this irritated the Rebels. When they left, the Rebels forced him to accompany them to Stanleyville.

Mayambi was not put into prison with the Belgians and Americans, but was placed under house arrest at the residence of the Congolese Catholic bishop. After three days he explained his situation to the prelate, and was permitted to return to his family.

One Sunday morning early in November, while Mayambi was preaching at the local church, Rebel soldiers surrounded the building. Their leaders then entered and accused Mayambi of being against the rebellion. Afterward they beat Mayambi and the other student who was leading the meeting, taking the other student with them when they left.

After two days in bed recovering from the beating, during which Mayambi became increasingly concerned for the other student, who had not returned, he arose and made his way to the Rebel headquarters where the friend was being held. After talking to the leader, Mayambi was permitted to take the other student back with him.

Most of the local people were thoroughly frightened by this time, and fled, leaving the students alone at the station.

When November 24 came, word quickly reached Banjwadi of the Stanleyville attack by paratroopers. Immediately Mayambi, his wife and children slipped away from the station, crossed the river, and went deep into the jungle. The other student and his wife accompanied them. Before long, they left the beaten paths and with difficulty entered a virgin area. There they made crude shelters and began a refugee existence.

For almost five months they remained hidden in their jungle retreat, gradually becoming aware of other refugees who were also hiding. Shoes and clothing wore out, they grew weary of the limited jungle diet and of the need for constant watchfulness against jungle animals. Still they remained. Yet, even so, they had no serious illness during those months.

Finally, in April, 1965, an informer led Rebels to the place where the refugees were hidden. They were forced to return to Banjwadi, by now a Rebel headquarters. Mayambi was forced to work as a clerk-typist. This was a dangerous, worrisome existence.

After two months, Mayambi gave himself up to a National Army patrol in the area, and arranged for the rescue of his family and others. This was accomplished, and after several weeks, Mayambi was permitted to go to Stanleyville with his family. There Pauline gave birth to their third son, whom she named John Baptist Misery — doubtless remembering the trials of the past nine months.

Here is what Mayambi says about their ordeal: "We are here because of the love and grace of God. I know that nothing happens to any of His children without His knowledge. Truly I had planned for four years of study at Banjwadi. I went to school for four years, all right, but the fourth year of study was much different than I had expected. The Lord decided to give me a year of schooling in the forest instead of in a classroom. It was a hard year but the Lord saw I needed it and I give Him thanks.

"I hope to complete my fourth year of theology training and then, if the Lord wills, continue my studies in a *faculte de theologie* (seminary). I have no other desire but to continue to prepare myself to serve my Lord and my church."

13/Prison Diary

AFTER THE VILLAGE of Kindu fell before the mercenaries' advance, a new spirit came over the captors. It was short-lived, but encouraging while it lasted. Word came to the missionaries that Colonel Opepe had gone to Roman Catholic confession. And the man immediately under the colonel, a Rebel major, came to the missionaries' room and asked Al Larson to pray with him. They sat on the bed together.

Simba guards brought gifts: razors and blades, bars of candy. It was obvious that they were afraid of what might happen if a rescue party arrived.

But the Simba propaganda medium, *The Martyr* (named in honor of Patrice Lumumba) warned that all hostages would be killed if any planes came over Stanleyville. "We'll cut up these people, we'll mutilate them, we'll torture them and then eat parts of their bodies," the paper warned. So the prisoners' joy at reports of the mercenary army's advance was tempered by fear of what might result if a rescue party actually arrived in Stanleyville.

Here are some entries from the small notebook-diary Charles Davis kept during his weeks of imprisonment at Hotel des Chutes. Many Bible passages which he mentions as a source of strength have been omitted for reasons of space.

NOVEMBER 1   "I sought the Lord, and he heard me, and delivered me from all my fears" (Psalm 34:4).

NOVEMBER 2   Meetings today to discuss letting the industries go back to work. Two plantation men are with us; they both pay over 600 workers on each place. Had occasion to open the Bible to them, and they listened while we had morning prayers. In God's grace we passed a peaceful night.

Have been reading *Pilgrim's Progress*. Bunyan's "Worldly Wisdom" tells Christian that if he continues in that way, among other things he is going to meet lions.

NOVEMBER 3   By the grace of God, we find ourselves still in Room 103. There are many worse places in Stan these days than Hotel des Chutes.

God has given us a host of promises today, and we had a good time of prayer. We have eaten well, and can only praise His name. One of the Belgians asked if he could read from *Pilgrim's Progress* tomorrow. What an opportunity.

"Delight thyself also in the Lord; and he shall give thee the desires of thine heart. Commit thy way unto the Lord; trust also in him; and he shall bring it to pass" (Psalm 37:4, 5).

This room is air-conditioned, and if it is not sufficient for seven men, still, we are in as comfortable a position as is possible in this town at present. Praise God for His goodness to His children.

Bunyan: "Stay in the middle of the path and the chained lions can do you no harm."

"Be not afraid of their faces: for I am with thee to deliver thee, saith the Lord" (Jeremiah 1:8).

NOVEMBER 4   Today we received Bibles for the other men in this room and they seem very pleased. We have had excellent points of contact with them. We trust now that with our testimony, the Word of God will sink deep roots into the hearts of these men.

An armored car just came into town. It is being used for propaganda now.

We just learned that Volker Gscheidle has gone out to be with the women. Praise God.

Tozer, in *Knowledge of the Holy*: "Wrong ideas about God are not only the fountain from which the polluted waters of idolatry flow; they are themselves idolatrous."

"Cyrus, He is my shepherd, and shall perform all my pleasure . . ." (Isaiah 44:28). If He could say this of the great Cyrus, what less control does He have here?

We received notes from Kilometer 8, and such joy to hear that all is well. Fear, Hector [McMillan] says, is a painful emotion arising from the expectation of evil. Oh, if we could only by grace dwell on the riches of His presence with us.

We have been having seasons of blessed prayer together. We know that all delays are in His hands. We are praying that Bob and Hector will be released. The house across the road has been emptied by the liberators.

"When thou liest down, thou shalt not be afraid: yea, thou shalt lie down, and thy sleep shall be sweet" (Proverbs 3:24).

(Many quotations from A. W. Tozer's *Knowledge of the Holy* are found in this section of the notebook.)

NOVEMBER 5   Read through I Pierre in French. This time in imprisonment has turned into blessing as God presses us into His Word.

Yesterday had time to finish *Pilgrim's Progress*. The scene of Christian arriving in Heaven makes one almost wish to go. How wonderful the meeting and the singing and the joy and the triumph must be at the arrival of the faithful.

There are many rumors in town today. The first is that meat and vegetables have arrived here. That was confirmed — we had some for dinner. The second is that the general [Olenga] has left town to go to the fight. This could be, for during the night we heard soldiers and trucks. But the third, unconfirmed, is one to beat them all: the Belgian government has moved two thousand paratroopers to a spot across the border and promises a rapid end to this confusion, if they hear of the death of a single European. We know that two Belgians were freed this morning. Praise God for small beginnings.

Mr. Lythurn had a baby boy last night — his wife, that is.

Today Florence Nightingale came with a few more clothes for the refugees. I got a lovely shirt and a pair of brown pants. God has been gloriously good to us in this time.

NOVEMBER 6 Had diarrhea most of the night. Probably from an overdose of good food.

NOVEMBER 7 Read Proverbs 7 and 8, and Psalm 31 for devotions this morning. "My times are in thy hand: deliver me from the hand of mine enemies, and from them that persecute me. . . . Be of good courage, and he shall strengthen your heart, all ye that hope in the Lord" (Psalm 31:15, 24).

After a night of sound sleep, we are all grateful for another day of grace. Last night Alonourd spoke a great deal about his background in a children's home. It certainly helps to understand a person if you know of the grace that overcame in his life.

Is the Congo finished? We have discussed some very interesting issues.

Concerning missionary deputation at home: The things that you have forgotten are the things that they want to hear. Bob [McAllister] insists that the approach at home is often backwards. The lack of missionaries in a given field may be God's chastisement on the church of that country. It is not necessarily the fault of the church at home.

Mr. Rambo [British consul] dropped in to visit us and thought he almost had his English charges [McMillan and McAllister] out of lock, but the Lord overruled, using the fears of the major who is in charge. He feared to release prisoners the colonel had put in bonds.

We learned that the prisoners who were brought back in had been beaten. This was, to say the least, very upsetting.

Troops have been moving all afternoon, probably to block an attack from the south. The Lions are becoming more and more dangerous as they are backed up. A cornered lion is always dangerous, but our God is the One who was able to close the mouths of the lions in Daniel's den.

Got a good supper, but the atmosphere has become very tight.

Al [Larson] just told me that we are to be sent out on the very first plane that arrives; but with the irrationality of the situation, it seems that only God can supply the fly-power.

NOVEMBER 8   Bob prayed this morning that the Lord would retain him here until *His* time. Just after that, the major came in and took the two British passports. Bob and Hector will soon be released.

Finished Tozer's book. He has placed me under terrific conviction regarding my low views of the Godhead. I thought I had the terminology when I left seminary to describe the greatness of God. But I don't any more. He's just too big.

I feel that I am learning something of the way God controls

history that I could never learn in seminary or in theological creeds. I find now that my vocabulary is totally inadequate to describe how powerful God is.

NOVEMBER 9   Today am reading an account of the Communist takeover of the church in China: *Come Wind, Come Weather*, by Leslie Lyall. I am humiliated by the courage of some of those Christian Chinese.

Much talk today of total release of the women. Much evil can be done in these next few days, so we must continue in stedfast prayer for all these people: Europeans and Congolese alike. There has been so much blood spilt already; if only a bloodless solution could now be found.

5:00 p.m.   The town is now deserted for the first time since our confinement. I heard a birdcall outside the window. The sky is heavily overcast with the gloomy condition of the war.

NOVEMBER 10   During the night, the electrical current was cut off for a long while. The women who were released during the night have been retaken.

There has been a great deal of optimism this morning, but in Congo all could change in a moment.

Merle [Chuck's name for Muriel] wrote this morning. Said that one of the consular staff had asked for a Bible from prison. Praise God.

Am now reading Isobel Kuhn's *Green Leaf in Drought Time*, in the French translation.

NOVEMBER 11   God has been bringing Himself glory from all this: (1) More Bibles sold because more money is available; (2) More baptisms and prayer; (3) Bo Martin willing to give his life for the women missionaries; (4) Death brings tremendous pressure on the African home — makes them turn to God; (5)

Missionaries are being tested to examine their relationship to the African; (6) The missionary is being forced to examine his own right to be here; (7) Stop taking so many things for granted; (8) Re-examine the importance of indigenous principles; (9) We have been forced to a fresh analysis of the field: *dawa*, witchdoctor, blood sacrifices, Simbas, cruelty.

After prayer this afternoon, rain began to fall. With the soft dripping against the window, it is hard to believe that an army is going to encircle this city. If only this war could end as gently as the rain clearing the dusty streets below.

NOVEMBER 12   During the night, they had an African here who was in trouble, but I was so tired I heard very little of the disturbance. It is a misty, rainy day. The town has little more activity than it's had the past several days.

In Muriel's letter yesterday, she said that Steve has developed a cough, and everyone now is scratching with this mysterious itch.

NOVEMBER 14   Quiet this morning. A couple of doctors were brought in from a great distance. They were 15 cruel days on the road. They saw no signs of an advancing government force.

My decision to take my family from all this madness is the only realistic one. By God's grace, I pray it shall be very soon.

NOVEMBER 18   Finished today the exciting story of Tom Sawyer in French.

We heard news today that three of the prisoners were brought to the Lumumba monument [where there had been many executions] and then were conducted back to the prison.

"We can easily forgive a child who is afraid of the dark. The real tragedy of life is when men are afraid of the light."

NOVEMBER 19 We were all changed today from Hotel des Chutes to Hotel Victoria, a much larger hotel. We three missionaries are still together. It was a wonderful thing to see so many wives find their husbands for the first time in weeks.

Have been thinking of Watchman Nee's words: "Whatever is given to God, He breaks — even as He broke the loaves and fishes. But in the breaking, He multiplies it."

14/Hotel Victoria

DURING THEIR 80-YEAR RULE, the Belgians made many indelible impressions on the Congolese. One was that it is not the government's job to feed prisoners; families have that responsibility.

But with Belgian and American families under house arrest at such places as Kilometer 8, or evacuated to Leopoldville, how were the prisoners of the Rebel army fed?

By heroic, unselfish Greeks.

Since Greece — unlike Belgium and the United States — had provided no aid to the National Government or mercenaries, the Greek population of Stanleyville was not under any regulation by the Simbas.

Free to move about the city at will, and to carry on their business, the Greeks could easily have avoided involvement with the imprisoned Belgians and Americans. Self-interest would surely have indicated the wisdom of such a course, especially when it meant dealing with people as unpredictable as the Simbas.

Instead, Greeks fed the prisoners, aided by individuals of a few other nationalities. They visited them, brought fresh clothing and medicine, and carried messages back and forth between the prisoners and their families.

To accomplish their humanitarian mission, and to prevent the burden from falling too heavily upon a few people, Stanleyville's Greeks formed a loose organization called *Les Central*. (Prisoners called it the White Cross.) Warehouses were already empty, so individuals contributed from their personal supplies to feed the 235 prisoners.

When a Greek drove up to Hotel Victoria with food, he was permitted by the Simba guards to distribute it on the four floors. Along with the food, he conveyed news and rumors (usually optimistic) to the prisoners. He also frequently brought messages from families on the outside. If the message was written and a guard was watching, it was "palmed" in a handshake.

Each floor had its own organization for food service. Belgians, "the best cooks in the world, in or out of prison," prepared the food. Occasionally its fragrance was so overpowering that a Simba risked the consequences of breaking *dawa* by taking some.

Chuck Davis remembers the day he first met Dr. Paul Carlson. It was at Hotel Victoria.

The missionaries heard that the famous prisoner had been brought from Central Prison to the hotel. Since they had been praying for him for the past two months, they were anxious to meet him. They were also anxious to have Christian fellowship with him, since they were sure he needed it as much as they did. And so three, including Chuck, sought him out the next morning (which was only four days before he died).

Because of the violence of the situation, and their common faith in Jesus Christ, a close fellowship was soon established. The little group of Christians came together a number of times during the next few days.

"Paul was a very practical person, very humble, quiet — almost timid." This is how Chuck remembers him. "Yet he was outgoing, friendly, very easy to get along with — even in an adverse situation. He looked awfully tired and haggard; of course, he'd been under the continuous threat of death for months.

"When we got to know him better, we kidded him about being a world figure now. We knew that he was front-page news in the United States and everywhere else. So we said that after he was back in the States, and met the President, we didn't want him to be too filled with pride, or he wouldn't be any use to himself.

"I guess he wasn't in the mood for any kidding. He took it seriously. 'I can't think of that,' he said. 'I can just live one day at a time, and trust the Lord for that day.'

"Actually, that was his attitude during those final days: 'Live one day at a time.'

"One time when we were talking, after he got to know us, Paul said something like this: 'I'd like to come back to the Congo. But this coming back would be a family decision. If my wife felt that we couldn't, I wouldn't force her into a situation like this. And my coming back — if we did — would be with certain conditions. We had an airstrip that was supposed to be built at our station. We're very isolated up there. I don't think we could come back without that airstrip being there for emergencies or possible evacuations in the future. If the airstrip had been there, we'd have had no difficulty leaving at the time trouble came. But it wasn't. It was just proposed — it was a future thing.' "*

---

*Less than a year after Dr. Carlson's death, the children in vacation Bible schools of the Evangelical Covenant and Evangelical Free churches (which cooperate in missionary work in the Wasolo area) collected money for an airplane for this station. An airstrip has since been built.

The missionaries at Hotel Victoria had frequent meetings for prayer. Because the Simbas were afraid of Christian praying, they didn't advertise the fact that they were meeting. And when they sang hymns, as they often did, they closed the windows. "It wasn't that we were ashamed of praying, or afraid," Chuck explains. "It was just that we decided to pray in a closet and expect God to answer openly."

Paul Carlson joined the little group on several occasions, when he could free himself from medical obligations.

"My major impression of Paul," Chuck says, "was hearing him pray. There was no formal organization of his prayers, no quoting Scripture. You know what I mean — like a professional Christian worker trained to pray in public a lot. You try to follow a certain pattern and fit your praying into that pattern.

"But Paul's prayers were nothing like that. They were very simple. He prayed like a person talking to Someone he loved, or like a son talking to his Father. There was no 'Thee' or 'Thou' in them. Paul always said 'You' when he was talking to God. His sentences were very short: 'Thank You, God, for being with me today.'

"The one thing you knew was that Paul had a direct line. You knew he wasn't worried about his prayers fitting into a theological position, or even quoting Bible verses. He just expected God to hear him. Like I said, he just had a direct line, and it was beautiful. His praying was a wonderful experience for all of us.*

"The one I remember is this: 'Lord, I thank You for this day, and for allowing me to live in it. I pray that today I may be a good witness for Your Son.' "

---

*A Congolese pastor, writing to a missionary in America, in the wake of suffering described in this book, had this to say about Congolese Christians' experience in prayer: "We used to pray to the Lord. We don't any more. Now we just talk to the Lord."

What did the missionaries pray for during these uncertain days? Chuck Davis answers.

"Grace to endure what we were going through. We didn't pray, 'Lord, get me out of here.' But we did pray for a peaceful settlement of the Rebel problem, even when this seemed to become more and more remote. We knew that God is not pleased with bloodshed.

"We also prayed for individual men and women in the non-missionary group, especially the Belgians who had never been reached with the Gospel of Christ. We really became concerned for these people in prison, and were so thankful when they listened to our witness, and accepted Bibles, and a few made profession of faith in Christ.

"We prayed a lot for the Congolese churches, too. We knew that the Christians were getting a lot of criticism and even persecution. And it was difficult for them to come together in groups. So we prayed for the churches. We knew the dangers they faced."

Since many of the prisoners were in poor health, and some were elderly, Dr. Paul Carlson organized a pool of medical supplies from which the several doctors could draw for treatment. The older men and women suffered most, although all had a touch of dysentery at one time or another. Or it may have been simple diarrhea (which Chuck Davis says was his condition), caused by drinking Cokes made from unpurified water. (In the absence of Belgian managers, Congolese were running many of Stanleyville's factories — something that had previously been dismissed with a shrug as "impossible.")

Hotel Victoria was a welcome change for all the prisoners, whether they were brought in from Central Prison (as were Dr. Carlson and most of the American consular staff), or army prison camps (most of the Belgians), or even from the relatively comfortable Hotel des Chutes.

For all, security regulations were relaxed in Hotel Victoria. Prisoners made their way from floor to floor, talking and exchanging experiences. Americans were impressed with the unconquerable optimism of the Belgians. Rumors started at the top floor and worked their way down to the bottom, where they were barely recognizable. Or they started at the bottom and went, floor by floor, to the top: American (or Belgian) troop planes were on their way. The prisoners would be released without any fighting at all. The Simbas would be leaving some night soon, pulling up stakes, and they'd be gone in the morning. Colonel Opepe had defected to the Nationalist Army with a number of his officers. — These were some of the wishful rumors.

On those rare occasions when troops were in the halls, and a lot of guns were around, the prisoners stayed in their own rooms. But the minute the Simbas left, the halls were again a place of running to-and-fro and excited conversation.

Saturday night, November 21, an unexpected order was shouted by the Simbas. It reverberated down the halls: "All men downstairs! All men downstairs!" This was around nine o'clock.

When all the male prisoners had gathered on the first floor, the Simba officer in charge of the building gave a long speech about American and Belgian atrocities. Their planes, he said, had bombed the town of Banalia, killing three colonels, two majors, and murdering most of the women and children in the area. General Olenga was furious with the prisoners, he said, and they were to be shipped to prison in the morning.

Some of the Americans noticed a peculiar lack of emotion in the officer as he spoke, an absence of the sort of feeling that usually accompanied anger in a Congolese. Comparing notes later, they felt that he was almost smiling behind the harsh words. Could this be one of the "jokes" which they were fond of playing on the prisoners?

They hoped it was, for his concluding words were, "All you men are to be moved to the prison tomorrow. There you will be shot. Now go back upstairs and be ready to move. Get your bedroll and wait in the hallway."

As they waited in the halls of the upper floors, most of the prisoners were upset over this latest development. There was always insecurity in being moved around, and some — like Paul Carlson—had already experienced repeated beatings and forced marches, even death sentences with last-minute commutations.

An hour passed, while the Simbas paraded up and down the halls, brandishing their weapons, threatening to bring their rifles down on prisoners' heads. Yet a feeling persisted that they were only playing a game.

A Simba would point his rifle at one of the men and look at him with his fierce eyes. ("Looking at them was like looking into the eyes of death, sometimes," Chuck Davis says. "But I recalled how the Lord told Jeremiah, 'Don't be afraid of their faces.'") If the prisoner stared back without flinching, the Simba would move away.

The high degree of tension and fear had its effect as the night wore on, for Dr. Carlson and his colleagues were called on to treat several older people with heart difficulties before morning.

For six hours, until three-thirty Sunday morning, the harassment went on. Still, the prisoners hadn't yet been shipped out to the prison.

At this time the Simbas seemed to lose interest, and some of the prisoners unrolled their bedrolls and stretched out on the hall floors. Chuck Davis was one who did.

"About an hour later, someone came along and gave me a kick in the side," Chuck recalls. "It didn't mean anything, it was just to wake me up. Then this Simba told me to go to my room. So I went back to the room and went to sleep. The whole affair had been a game; there'd been no bombing at Banalia or anywhere else. They were just having fun at our expense.

"You felt all the time as if a cat-and-mouse game was going on. You never knew when things were serious and when they weren't. This was their way of keeping themselves amused."

But that Sunday afternoon was a different story. Two trucks and a bus were brought to Hotel Victoria, and all the male prisoners were herded aboard. Destination was announced as Banalia, which had supposedly been bombed.

The bus, crowded with almost a hundred men, was suffocating. Inevitably, some became sick when the trip to Banalia had hardly begun. But suddenly, at Kilometer 12 (about seven miles out), the bus broke down. It wouldn't budge. So the passengers had to be brought back to Hotel Victoria in other vehicles, where they were two days later when Belgian and American rescue troops arrived.

"The whole affair reminded me of Psalm 21:11," Chuck Davis says. " 'They imagined a mischievous device, which they are not able to perform.' "

15/Massacre at Banalia

Bo Martin and Assani Benedict are twins. When they were small, they wondered about the Creator who had made everything they saw around them.

When the twins were old enough to go to school, they were accepted at Banalia mission school. Those were happy years, especially after they both came to know Jesus Christ through an aged Congolese saint, Andre Yengo. It seemed the right next step for them was to yield their lives and service to Jesus Christ.

Their training days at Bongondza Bible School were soon over, and they were prepared with a solid background in the Bible for the work they felt God wanted them to do: evangelize their own tribe.

The twins were hard workers. And they were enthusiastic. Both qualities were necessary as they traveled from village to village, preaching, exhorting at night sessions around campfires. They organized small groups of believers into churches, they trained assistants to preach in the outlying areas, until the whole area had heard the Gospel and hundreds had accepted the Saviour.

New churches were started in a score of villages, and buildings were constructed. But the village church at Bopepe was the leader; on Sundays, hundreds of Christians marched singing to the central church, to worship there.

Bopepe soon became a station of the Unevangelized Fields Mission. Miss Mary Baker, a graduate of Moody Bible Institute, was assigned by the mission to be the first resident missionary. Because of the sort of woman Mary Baker was, her presence did not change the nature of this unusual indigenous church.

The village had at its center a spacious church building, built by the Christians who settled at Bopepe. (It was a rarity in the Congo, or anywhere else, for that matter: a Christian village.) Bopepe was a place of clean, bright homes, gorgeous flowers, and happy children. A school and dispensary were located there.

Pastors and evangelists went out from Bopepe to evangelize the surrounding country. Bo Martin was their leader; he lived in Bopepe with his wife and children. So did Assani, his twin; the two were close in the Lord's work.

The Christians at Bopepe built a house for Mary Baker. Shortly after the Congo's independence, Margaret Hayes was also appointed to the village, to provide medical service. The missionaries' house was in constant use, and the Congolese were always welcome — for a cup of coffee, a glass of water, or just to talk.

Mary and Margaret were two missionaries who didn't try to preserve a color line between themselves and the Congolese. Another missionary recalls the visit of Mary's pastor, the Reverend Richard Seume of Richmond, Virginia, to Bopepe:

"I was invited to stay with Mary during that time, and we

made visits to the outlying churches together in her new car. Pastor Assani was the driver.

"As we returned one evening from a visit to a plantation, we passed a Congolese family on the road. The mother was loaded with a heavy basket on her back, the father likewise had baggage and a bunch of spears tied together, and there were three small children.

"Pastor Assani stopped the car. 'These are our people, we must help them,' he announced.

"We all got out, and into the back of the car climbed mother, children, and her packages, some of them smelling strongly of dried meat. With difficulty the spears were fixed in the bottom of the car, regardless of the comfort of the passengers. Then everyone else was packed in and we continued on home.

"It was Mary's car, a new one, too. And it was a special occasion, when Pastor Seume was on a visit. But Assani never asked permission to bring the passengers aboard — all was taken for granted. The party arrived safely and gratefully at Bopepe. What a revelation of the grace of God in His child.

"Walking with Pastor Seume that evening, I remarked that there were many missionaries who were not so Christlike as to allow their property to be used to serve any and everyone without their permission. To me it was another glimpse of the Master, who Himself went about doing good."

But the days of peace at Bopepe were numbered, for the Simba rebellion was closing in on that part of the Congo.

A few weeks before the storm broke, Mary Baker wrote to a friend in Ireland: "Pastor Assani is away at the moment with his family — his wife has been ailing for some time and now he has taken her to the third doctor. We feel that perhaps his having been away so much has made the burden on her with the family too heavy. Do be much in prayer, for more and more Assani is being called away for ministry — all over the Congo, and even farther afield. We thank God for the gift that He has given to Assani, and his love for the Word, and his devotion to the Saviour and the Gospel."

Thus Assani, Bo's twin, was away from Bopepe when the Simbas came.

The following description of what happened to the missionaries, and to the church at Bopepe, was written by Bo Martin:

Beloved brothers in Jesus Christ, I wish to tell you a little of what happened here to us at the time of the rebellion. I wish to tell you of the death of our missionaries in the territory of Banalia, and also how God saved me. Praise and grace be to our God, the Father of Jesus Christ our Lord. He does with us His children according to His will. Whether life or death for us, His children, it comes from the hand of the Lord.

"For none of us liveth to himself, and no man dieth to himself. For whether we live, we live unto the Lord; and whether we die, we die unto the Lord: whether we live therefore, or die, we are the Lord's. For to this end Christ both died, and rose, and revived, that He might be Lord both of the dead and living" (Romans 14:7-9).

On the 4th of August, 1964, the Rebels took Stanleyville. Not many days later, they came to our territory of Banalia. Then one day they came to our station at Bopepe to search, to see if we had any guns, or whether we had hidden any of the soldiers of the National Army. Not one gun or one soldier did they find with us. They took only the radio transmitter away with them. They also scattered the belongings and papers which they found in the missionaries' homes. Again and again, when they returned to the station, they scattered the things about in this manner. I believe they did this in all our mission stations.

Since the Rebels were enemies of the white people, and we were friends of the missionaries, they began to call us "Americans." At that time much hatred came upon us, with bitter threats and accusations against us.

In November, 1964, a telegram came from Stanleyville telling the Rebel leaders that they should arrest all whites, but not to harm them. At two o'clock in the morning the Rebels came to Bopepe to arrest Miss Baker, Miss Hayes and me. These Simbas were kind to us, and they let the ladies rest quietly until the morning. I slept with the Simbas on the veranda.

In the morning they took us to Banalia on foot. This was 22 kilometers [14 miles] away. At five o'clock that afternoon we arrived at Banalia, and the ladies were exhausted. The Simbas took us before their leaders, who said that an order had been received to take us all to Stanleyville. There we would appear before their General Olenga.

After long questioning and accusations, they asked for the ladies' passports. After this they took the ladies to a house where many other whites from the plantations were being held. In that building they were imprisoned.

Since there were no beds in that house, I tried to find beds for our missionaries to sleep on that night. When the Simbas saw me doing this, they were furious with me. They took me to their leader, saying, "This Pastor Bo Martin is hunting a bed to give the whites imprisoned here, that they may sleep upon a mattress!"

Immediately their leaders sent them to throw me into the prison. They came quickly, took me by the neck, and said, "Today, you friend of the whites, you will see!" They made me run very fast and threw me into prison.

That night all our missionaries slept on the bare cement floor. That day they had also brought in the Parrys. Mrs. Parry was sick with fever, and her body was weak and ill.

The next day they sent all the other whites to Stanleyville. Those who remained were only Dr. Sharpe and his family; Mr. and Mrs. Parry and their children; Miss Mary Baker and Miss Margaret Hayes; Miss Gray; and three Catholic sisters and a priest. We Congolese imprisoned there with them were Philippe Masini, Mbongo Samuel and myself.

After a day, they freed me to get food for all of us who were imprisoned there. I did this, and the churches at Banalia and Bopepe sent food day after day to feed their brethren in prison.

In the midst of the prison, the missionaries at all times rejoiced. They said to me that death is good for us who are Christians. Their faces were shining with the Glory of the Lord.

The Simba chiefs gave Dr. and Mrs. Sharpe, Miss Hayes and Miss Gray work to do in the hospital. They were doing that work with joy and with a very good heart. Miss Baker continued to do her work of keeping the mission records as she had always done.

Here are the last words and testimony of each of them, which they often said, before they died:

Miss Baker: "Bo Martin, I am now 50 years old; and in all my life the Lord Jesus has kept me wonderfully. I am very happy to go to dwell with Him there in Heaven. Father and mother are Christians; father died in Christ and is now with the Lord in Heaven. Thus I am keenly desirous to go to be with them there on high."

Dr. Sharpe: "There in Heaven, doctors aren't needed, for there is no illness. Doctors will have no work there."

Mr. Parry: "Bo Martin, do you know the history of the Church?"

I replied, "Yes, Bwana."

Another time, he asked whether I knew the story of Polycarp.

Again I replied, "Yes, Bwana."

Then he asked me, "The end of his life — how was that?"

I replied that his enemies arrested him, accused him, and said, "If you will renounce Jesus and curse Him, we will release you from prison and spare your life." Polycarp replied to his enemies, "I have served my Lord Jesus many years. He has never done me evil — not even once! How could I deny Him now? I could never deny my Lord." So Polycarp's enemies burned him in the fire.

Then Bwana Parry said to me, "Now it has come to be my turn. God does not want Christians to waver in times of grief or pain. We must be like Polycarp, strong soldiers of Jesus Christ. In other lands the blood of many Christians has been spilt, and in some, the blood of missionaries. Here in Congo, the blood of Christians has not yet been poured out. Thus it is as if God wills that our blood be poured out here in Congo. But the great thing is this: God does not want Christians to turn back in times of pain and suffering. I believe that you will never waver. Stand firm. Be strong and brave."

After one week with them at Banalia, I went to Bopepe to find food for them. I was there three days when I saw Simbas entering the village with the mission car. Miss Hayes was with them. They said that their chiefs and the whole population there had agreed to return Miss Hayes to the mission to do her work of caring for the sick, and maternity work. That was November 23, 1964. The next day, the National Army recaptured Stanleyville. So on the following day the Simbas said, "Let's kill all the white prisoners."

It was four o'clock in the afternoon when they began to kill the missionaries. They took Dr. Sharpe out of the operating theatre, without even permitting him to finish his work. The place where the massacre took place was before the ferry, beside the river Aruwimi.

They began by killing a Congolese, Albert Ajamba, who was president of an opposing party. When they brought Dr. Sharpe, they said to him, "We will kill just your family and we will leave you to serve us in the hospital."

"I will die together with my family," the doctor said to them. "It is best if you kill me first."

Quickly one Simba pierced him with a spear, then they beat him with guns and arrows. After they had killed the doctor, they killed Mrs. Sharpe, and finally their children.

After that they killed Mr. and Mrs. Parry and their children. And then Miss Baker and Miss Gray. Finally, they killed the three Catholic sisters and the priest.

They threw all the bodies into the river.

This was the end of the life of our missionaries who died here in Congo and in the territory of Banalia. Now they are resting with complete joy with the Lord there in Heaven.

Fifteen years before she was killed by the Simbas, Mary Baker wrote the following account of an incident that was a great encouragement to her:

Frances Longley and I were sitting at the table in the living room, putting the final touches on preparation for the next day, which was Sunday. It was late.

Suddenly we were startled to hear someone come bounding up on the veranda — all three steps in one leap. A hurried knock on the door followed.

There is only one person around who runs and jumps like that: Denys, the teacher at our boys' school. But we couldn't imagine why he would appear at that hour on Saturday night.

Frances went to the door and invited the teacher in. In his quick way, he bounded around to the place where he usually sits when he visits us, and sat down on the very edge of the chair.

What could be wrong? Neither of us asked the question, but I could almost hear Frances thinking it.

Denys panted a moment or two, then began to talk. "Oh, Miss," he said, speaking to Frances, "I have no peace tonight. The Lord has been speaking to my heart about a matter, and I just can't seem to rest until I tell you about it.

"It's about the church. We just can't let you purchase those leaves and then pay workmen to put them on the church building." — We knew what he was talking about. The building in which we worshiped was in bad condition, and the roof had become steadily worse until it now leaked so badly that the least little shower sent us all flying to our houses.

"If we let the people in your country pay for a thing like that, we are the laziest people on earth. Worse than that, we lie when we sing about how much we love Christ, and we will be sinning a great sin in the eyes of God."

I don't think either of us had a word to say, we were so surprised by this opening announcement of what the Lord had been putting into the heart of our African fellow worker.

The teacher continued. "We Christians on the station and in the villages around here can do that job if we want to. I know it isn't my turn to preach tomorrow, but may I not do it, for my heart is full of a message for my people?"

Like two proud mothers, we fairly beamed: our children, to whom God had sent us, were going to do the very thing we had secretly hoped for in our hearts. They were going to arise and build just for their love for Him.

We couldn't hold back any longer, so Frances told the

teacher we had wanted that very thing to happen, but we knew the suggestion must come from them. Otherwise it would have been coercion from the white missionaries and not a real labor of love for God. So before Denys went home, we talked and looked up Scriptures and prayed. After he left, Frances and I talked about how wonderfully God works.

On Sunday Denys preached. For two hours he poured out his heart to a full church. What did he say for two hours? I shall try to tell you, but I can only say that I was sorry when the end came. We two missionaries were privileged that day to see what God can do in an African's life.

He started with Moses and told how he had built the Tabernacle in the wilderness, according to God's pattern. That tent was their church building to remind them that Jehovah was always near, and that He traveled with them. The people came there to worship and receive cleansing. Next he explained about David and Solomon, and how the Temple was built. Then he told about the people's sin, Hezekiah's call to repentance, and the renewal of services in the Temple. Denys explained the people's rejection of God again, how they were led into captivity, and then how Nehemiah rebuilt the Temple.

From the New Testament, Denys read passages that told of God's other temples: our Lord's own body, the body of every believer. But he reminded us that God does not dwell in temples made with hands — Heaven is God's throne and the earth is His footstool.

All the while, he was driving home the point that a temple raised to God, whatever form it might take, must be guarded with a holy zeal; it is a place, a thing of honor and praise to the God of this universe.

I think the most dramatic part of his message was when he told the story of Simon of Cyrene, whom they "compelled" to bear the cross of Christ.

"Compelled," he said. "A black man compelled to bear the Saviour's cross. He is a disgrace to our race for all generations. Could he not have carried it because of his love for the One who would hang upon it and die for even his sins? Why did he have to be compelled?

"And why should the white man forever be bearing us as his burden? Have we no love for our Saviour? Cannot we bear a load this coming week for Him?

"If we allow the white man to pay to have this house repaired," Denys continued, "we are filled to overflowing with laziness, and we shall be accounted as terrible sinners in the sight of God. What shall we do?"

At that point he called on everybody — the monitors of his school, the 125 or so lads of his classes, the men in the class for evangelists, the women, the villagers, the workmen, the several tribes represented — to say what they would do.

Without exception, the reply was a loud and joyful, "We will arise and build!" Immediately he announced that all other work would be suspended for the coming week, and every head and heart and body would be thrown into the task.

The next three days our people, young and old, men and women, all walked a distance of at least eight miles, cut bundles of leaves, put loads of up to a hundred pounds on their backs, walked back the eight miles, unloaded, and then went back for another load.

An old father, who lives in almost a dog house, went along with the rest and cut his bundles. The task was too hard for him, and he was sick the next day — but a happy old man just the same.

Denys worked as hard as anybody else.

Today I watched our people work down at the church building. Almost the entire roof had to be taken down in order to replace some of the larger beams which had been eaten by ants.

The main upright poles had veered a bit off center. So with heavy forest vines, they tugged the poles back into position as I held my breath for fear the whole building would topple over on them.

How they all worked. Tonight, when they stopped, the roof was well over half-covered with leaves again. That includes replacing a number of poles, tying on reeds to which the leaves are attached, and preparing the leaves to go on.

The 125 school boys have carried a heavy part of the work today. They are well trained and know how to work.

The job will not be done until some mudding is done and the walls are again whitewashed, but the Christians will see the job through. We believe God is going to bless them for the love they have shown through the labor of their hands.

Have some shirked?

Yes, a few. But we forget these few when we think of the tiny fellow today who was making trip after trip with leaves on his head — loads far heavier than his own body — with terrible sores on both feet, and every step a limp. My heart nearly broke at the sight.

I finally called him from the task, brought him to the house, bathed his sores and doctored them. Then I gave him a glass of milk and a piece of candy to delight his heart. He is a precious lad and loved his task — so willingly he worked.

There was a hunchback woman from the village, too. She brought her load of leaves today. Perhaps not too big a bundle, but she gave her all.

Some folks feel sorry for the two of us alone at this village; we think God has specially blessed us and touched many hearts.

16/The Lieutenant's Dream

ONLY ONE of the captured missionaries had escaped death in the Banalia massacre. That was Margaret Hayes, who a short time before had been permitted to return to Bopepe in response to the villagers' pleas for her medical services.

When news of the deaths reached Bo Martin, who was also at Bopepe, he determined to hide Miss Hayes in the tropical forest. Otherwise, the Simbas would find her and kill her as well.

Here is what happened, in Bo Martin's words:

In the forest we were able to eat well, for we were in the gardens of our villagers. We slept in huts. Daily we prayed earnestly that God would save us from the hands of the enemy.

While we were in the forest, our enemies constantly accused us to the Simbas, saying that the Bopepe people had fled with a white person and were hiding her in the forest. That was indeed a difficult time for all the people at Bopepe: many threats toward us, quietness no longer ours, daily expecting only death.

At such times we lingered long in prayer.

Great troubles came to Bopepe on December 21, 1964. The Simbas took everything they could find, took out all the beds, chairs, cupboards, etc., and burned these things, together with all the houses.

While some were wrecking the village, other Simbas entered the forest to try to find the place where we were hiding Miss Hayes. On their way, they found our evangelist, Henri Alumba. They tied his hands together and began to beat him so hard that he almost died. When the mission people heard him crying out for help, they quickly came to help him. A fierce fight ensued. Miss Hayes and I could hear it in the place where we were hiding. I suggested to Miss Hayes that we throw ourselves down on the ground and pray to God that He save our people in that fight.

The Simbas had guns and spears. But the Christians had only spears and arrows of iron.

When the Simbas saw that the men of the mission came with great strength and courage to rescue their brother, they began to fire their guns fiercely. The men of the village weren't afraid, but shouted at the Simbas and chased them until they were in full flight. Then they left Henri Alumba in his ropes and chased them with all their might.

Soon they caught a Simba who had a gun, and then caught four others. The mission men did not wish to kill any of the Simbas, though the Simbas had killed many; because they were Christians they feared to spill blood.

Truly, that day we saw the power of God! Not one of our men died, or even received a wound. That fight took place in the forest.

When night came, Miss Hayes and I returned to the hut where we were hiding. We found that they had tied up the Simba with strong ropes. They asked us what they should do with him. I warned them that as we are Christians, we could certainly not kill the man. They all agreed, saying, "If we had wanted to kill him before, then you would not have found him here!" Then we untied him and let him go, although we kept his gun.

Since it was now night, we did not find the women and children, for they had feared the noise of the guns and scattered into the forest. So each man went his own way into the night to call and hunt for his family. There was great confusion and trouble for us all that day, for no one knew where his relatives were. I was the same as the rest: I did not know where my wife and children were.

Miss Hayes and I went together, we walked all night through the jungle. We ate nothing for a whole day, and truly, we were utterly weary. We could not rest very well, for we had no blankets. Each one was trying to fold his arms about himself like a bird because of the night coldness.

Before I slept, I read the little Gospel of John which was in my pocket, for I had a small lantern. I no longer had a Bible.

In the morning, because we had heard that the National Army had come to Banalia to find and rescue the whites, we began to cut through the forest to try to reach them, hoping that they would save us. We were in that forest three days trying to find our way through it to Banalia. Even there, in the midst of the forest, they told us that the National Army had come to Banalia to rescue the white people, but they had passed on.

We no longer knew what we could do; we had come to the end of our wisdom.

A heavy rain beat upon us that night as we were walking. We found a little building and entered it, even in the night, and I hunted wood and lit a fire with matches that I had guarded very carefully. So we crouched near the fire to dry the clothes that were on us, for we had no other clothes to put on and no blankets to wrap around us. Miss Hayes' sandals were all torn to pieces, our feet were badly swollen, and our bodies were covered with sores. That day we suffered greatly.

The next morning I saw that our strength was almost gone because of the many privations and sufferings. I said to Miss Hayes, "Please, let us not die here in the jungle. It is better that we die in the village. God knows what to do for us, His children."

Miss Hayes agreed that it would be well for God to work His will for us.

Near the village, we met a young man, and I put Miss Hayes into his care to take her out of the forest to his father, the chief.

Before we parted, we prayed with tears. I said to Miss Hayes, "Go well, and I will follow you later."

That youth led Miss Hayes to the chief, and the chief took her to a major of the Simbas. When the major saw Miss Hayes, he said, "I will not kill you. Since you are a nurse, you will remain to help us." So he gave her the work of being their nurse. This was not the major who killed our missionaries, but another one.

Not many days later, I also came out to the major. When the Simbas saw me coming out of the forest, they all yelled "Butter! Butter!" which is their way of warning a person that they're going to kill him. "You!" they shouted at me, "You who hide white people, you will certainly die!" And one of them struck me on the face.

For two weeks they tried my case. They questioned me closely, to find out if I was Assani, my twin — "who goes to Europe to sell Congo to the Americans!"

I replied, "No, I am his brother."

They said, "If you were Assani, we would not hear your case, we would kill you at once. Since you are not Assani, we will give you a trial."

Others said, "Even though you are not Assani, you will die a painful death."

But others said, "He is not worthy of death."

One day, many of them said with oaths that tomorrow I was to die. That night I prayed earnestly to God, saying, "Father God, I put my life in Your hands. Death or life, I cannot choose, but do for me as You alone will."

In the morning, a Simba lieutenant came to get me at the prison. I thought surely my death had come and I was going to the Lord.

He took me to his office, and said, "Father Pastor, forgive me. I am the man who has pushed greatly for you to die. But this night I could not sleep very much. A person unseen accused me sternly, saying, 'Why do you wish to kill my messenger?' Because of this you will not die."

Then the lieutenant called others, to tell them what he had seen in the night. They all agreed that I should be released. They gave me permission to return to my village openly, in the sight of all men, and of the Simbas also. Many Simbas wondered, "Why do they not kill that man?"

I returned to my village praising God, with great joy for the way in which He had saved me from the hands of my enemies.

When I returned home, I found my wife and all our children safe and well. They were staying with one of our evangelists. Then my wife and children went to rest a while with her mother. After a few days I went to get them to bring them home. When I arrived there, the people accused me to the Simbas, saying I had killed 12 Simbas at Bopepe.

They imprisoned me again and for three days questioned me sharply. Then one Simba who had been at Banalia when I was being tried stood up and said, "That is a lie. I was there when they tried this pastor at Banalia. Even our biggest chief there freed him." So once more they gave me permission to return home.

I came back to my village, but again fled into the forest, for my enemies were still seeking to harm me. In all, I remained in the forest five months.

On June 2, 1965, the National Army again took Banalia. Someone told them that the pastor of Bopepe, together with his people, were hiding in the forest, and said he knew where we were. So 12 soldiers were sent by their lieutenant with the person who knew where we were, to bring us out of the forest. They brought us out to Banalia, where the National Army cared for us.

At the time of the rebellion, my brother Assani was in the hospital at Oicha because his wife was ill. He fled into Uganda. On August 20, 1965, he came here to Stanleyville. When he arrived, he came quickly to get me at Banalia, to bring me to Stanleyville with my family. When I saw my brother again, we rejoiced together with surpassing joy because God had saved us and guarded us in all this trouble. We and our families are living together and praising our Lord.

There are many of our young people, who were in U.F.M. schools together, here in Stanleyville. We are again instructing them in the Word of God, and are seeking to bring others to Christ.

I am filled with praise and thankfulness every day toward our Father God, because He has saved some of us in the time of the rebellion in Congo. In the midst of all this, we can say as Paul, our brother, said: "We are troubled on every side, yet not distressed; we are perplexed, but not in despair; persecuted, but not forsaken; cast down, but not destroyed; always bearing about in the body the dying of the Lord Jesus, that the life also of Jesus might be made manifest in our body. . . . For our light affliction, which is but for a moment, worketh for us a far more exceeding and eternal weight of glory; while we look not at the things which are seen, but at the things which are not seen: for the things which are seen are temporal; but the things which are not seen are eternal" (II Corinthians 4: 8-10, 17, 18).

17/Margaret and the Nuns

THE MAGNIFICIENT Margaret Hayes is British. She lived through the London Blitz and trained as a nurse in a bombed London hospital.

Her British character and Christian depth doubtless explain Margaret's survival in the tropical forest with Bo Martin, and her courageous decision to give herself up to the Simbas.

Why did she surrender, when she fully expected to be tortured and killed as had the others at Banalia? Not because life in the forest was too hard for her; she could have lasted indefinitely. Rather, her brave decision was made to save the lives of Christians at Bopepe who had protected the two fugitives and fed them during their weeks of hiding.

When they heard rumors that a white woman was being sheltered by the Christians at Bopepe, the Simbas were furious. They swept into the little village, killed two Christians and burned homes. When these actions did not make the Christians lead them to Margaret Hayes, the Simbas issued an ultimatum: either the white woman would be surrendered to them, or the whole Christian church would be executed.

The two who were killed were brothers of Bo Martin and Assani Benedict, the twins.

When she heard this by the jungle grapevine, Margaret's mind was made up. She would surrender and die, rather than be responsible for the death of other believers. (Bo Martin may believe that his suggestion led to Miss Hayes' decision because Margaret didn't tell him her real reason.)

And so, on Christmas Eve of 1964, she walked out of the jungle and gave herself up.

Surprisingly, the Simbas didn't kill her. Perhaps their fury had abated, perhaps her great act of self-sacrifice held back their spears. More likely, it was their critical need of medical help, and the fact that Margaret was a nurse.

Her captors took Margaret to Banalia and Bengamisa, where she nursed the sick and wounded for a time. Then the Simbas moved her north to Buta; there she was imprisoned at a Roman Catholic convent with 31 priests, 15 nuns, and a Belgian woman and her two children.

Meanwhile, back in England, the Unevangelized Fields Mission authorities and her family and friends believed that Margaret was dead. She was included in the memorial service at London's Westminster Chapel, "missing, believed dead."

But several rumors came out of the Congo that Margaret Hayes was still living. And then, in March, 1965, a letter was received from Margaret herself. Somehow, in that isolated Simba outpost of Buta, she had managed to get a letter into the post.

The only address was "Congo." The letter said that she was well, that she had enough to eat, and that the others had indeed all died at Banalia. "Only I am left," she said in closing.

Two more letters reached London that spring. One mentioned her fortieth birthday: "Today I have reached the awful age and, reading Deuteronomy 8:1-10, I was very amused, but how true it is that the Lord has led me these forty years. His hand has surely been upon me for good, yes, even in the trials, even in the wilderness, He was with me in it all, to prove me and to humble me. Oh that it may bring forth the fruit *He* desires.

"The sisters presented me with a magnificent bouquet at breakfast, plus a birthday card and a present. You'd never think we were prisoners-of-war! Several priests came over and gave their greetings, too. Truly the fellowship of suffering is a very precious fellowship, for it sweeps away all barriers of language, color and creed. Philippians 3:10 reveals the wish that we may be in fellowship with the sufferings of the Lord, but what He allows us to suffer is nothing to what He bore for us; even so, it is a privilege to have been allowed to go through these difficult days, for He has become so very much more precious; sometimes it is necessary for Him to remove *all* human props in order that we may better lean on Him who alone is able to support us at these times.

"Apart from my Bible, the only other book I possess is what I found at Banjwadi, *God Holds the Key*, by Geoffrey Bull [an account of his experience with God during imprisonment under the Chinese Communists]. Have found strange comfort in Mr. Bull's writings, and the meditations are a source of great blessing to my heart. He understands how I feel now, and in moments of distress I've turned again and again to the book when it had been difficult to pray, etc."

The next time Margaret wrote, and the letter arrived in England, was the occasion of her parents' golden wedding anniversary. "Again opportunity is given to send you word that all is well with me here, and the Lord is providing for our needs in a wonderful way. Praise Him! There has been a real break for me spiritually, and truly I am experiencing more and more the consciousness of His abiding presence; I guess it is that you folk at home are praying.

"Days pass very quickly, there is usually enough to occupy one's hands during the day, and we go to bed early. I'm making epaulettes for the 'Army'; I had to wrap them in pairs, so since I came here first as a missionary and secondarily as a prisoner, and not having a bean to my name, I asked the sisters for some small printed pictures of Christ. I chose some with Christ surrounded by people of all nations. So now each packet goes out with one of these in it; if only the recipient would turn his thoughts to Christ and pray for pardon and peace!

"The 22nd April was my parents' golden wedding (I don't know if they're still alive). However, the sisters went all out, and we celebrated royally, with poems written in English, and two songs in English (written by the priests).

"Would value your prayers for food; so far we have enough, but we've only enough flour left for another week (we bake bread for 57), and meat is getting low; the priests and brothers have been without meat for almost two weeks now.

"The Mother Superior has given me material to make a dress, and one of the priests also had two dresses in the attic left over from clothes sent for the 'poor of Congo'! These he graciously gave me, and we've altered them, so now I am decently dressed once again!

"There are numerous opportunities for prayer and meditation, and I specially remember No. 9 [address of the Unevangelized Fields Mission in London] and U.F.M. generally at 5:30 a.m. and again at 2:30-3:30 p.m. Midday, 6:30 and night I devote to the Congo field; these times are exceedingly precious to me, as you can guess.

"Mr. Harris, we can't leave our field high and dry! We *must* have workers, and if God wills, when and if I'm released, I would like to return. Think of the poor scattered flock of Christ! My heart breaks whenever I think of it.

"Two weeks ago I went down with a really severe attack of malaria and the sisters spoiled me; the Queen herself couldn't have had better treatment. This last week we've dysentery in the camp; I've had a light attack, but am now over it. A month ago we all weighed ourselves, and I have gained 20 lbs. out of the 30 that I lost!"

During Margaret's captivity in the convent, she made 1500 pairs of epaulettes. Each first Wednesday of the month, she followed the U.F.M. custom of praying for a half-day. The nuns didn't disturb her at this time; the custom made an impression on them.

Margaret's friends in England, and the mission authorities, knew that she was in desperate danger — especially as the mercenary army massed its forces for a drive to the north, to Buta. Christians in many lands prayed for God's brave child.

The commander of the Simba forces at Buta was a Congolese not yet thirty years old, Colonel Makondo. He was a fierce man, cruel toward his troops and seemingly without mercy.

When word came that the mercenary troops were on their way to Buta, Colonel Makondo ordered the massacre of the 31 priests in the convent. David W. Truby (*Congo Saga*) describes what happened:

"About eleven in the morning a mob of Simbas arrived armed with spears, shouting and yelling, and their intentions were obvious. Could it be that the mercenaries were already in shooting distance?

"The women locked the doors and turned out the lights, hoping to 'hold on' for a short while. But the Mother Superior ordered the doors to be opened and the ladies were marched over to the Fathers' quarters and then on to the postoffice building.

"The priests were taken from their quarters and brutally beaten. They took the beating very bravely, with scarcely a cry or shout, and the punishment lasted until four in the afternoon. They were then given the special Simba torture. Their arms were crossed behind their backs and tied at the elbows. Similarly, the legs were crossed and tied at the ankles and knees. Then a rope was passed around the elbows and ankles and the ankles were drawn up, forcing the body into a backward arch, into an extremely painful position. For the first time the priests cried in agony. Water was poured on the knots to make them fast; later the ropes were cut and they were marched to the river bank.

"A Simba stood at the door of the room where the ladies were held and gave a running commentary on the proceedings.

"The priests were then attacked with machetes, killed, and thrown into the river.

"The Simba guard passed one of the mutilated legs around and forced everyone to handle it. One of the children asked what sort of animal it was. Her mother replied she did not know, it was just 'something from the forest.' "

When the National Army and mercenaries did reach Buta, hoping to rescue the hostages held there, they found that another massacre had taken place, and that the women had disappeared.

Using the women as a shield, the Simbas had left Buta by the Basale Trail, a narrow path. When they had put enough distance between themselves and the mercenaries, they camped.

A new cruelty now characterized the Simbas' attitude toward the women. They were not allowed to pray; one nun caught with her hands clasped was roughly hit with the shaft of a spear: "There is only one god and that is Lumumba!" her attacker cried.

The women did not even dare to undress to bathe when led to the stream for that purpose. Surrounded by the ever-present guards, they dabbled in the water, fully clothed.

The situation must have seemed completely hopeless to Margaret and the nuns. They knew that even if a rescuing party of mercenaries approached, they would be slaughtered in reprisal, as had the priests.

A month of desperate, hopeless days passed. But the brave women maintained their morale, and God was working.

Then, after a month, a captured Congolese was forced to lead the rescue party to the Simbas' hideout. The National Army officer warned the mercenaries not to shoot, or "we will find only bodies, instead of people."

No sound of their approach alerted the guards. Margaret, lying quietly in her hut, was suddenly startled to see white legs charging toward her, to hear bursts of gunfire, cartridges falling on the roof, and the yelling of the mercenaries. The surprised and terrified Simbas fled.

It was all over in two minutes. They were rescued.

For months Margaret had endured depths of suffering, dreadful sights of torture and cruelty, without breaking down. Now, when she saw her rescuers, she wept.

Five years before, in England on furlough, a hymn had made a deep impression on Margaret. She remembers hearing it drift across a lovely park; she remembers, too, that tears came to her eyes as she thought of the Congo and her work there. That was 1960. Now she understands the hymn a little better:

If we could see, if we could know,
We often say;
But God in love a veil doth throw
Across our way.
We cannot see what lies before,
And so we cling to Him the more;
He leads us till this life is o'er:
Trust and obey.

18/The Ecumenism
of Suffering

MISSIONARY LIFE is, in many respects, characterized by isolation. The missionary may not want to be isolated, but he is usually powerless to prevent it.

In the Congo, missionaries were islands apart from the mainland of Belgian plantation life and American social activity. In their work and worship, missionaries were close to Congolese Christians, but they were isolated in other areas of life. And they were far more isolated from the non-Christian Congolese community.

But when other bridges are missing or destroyed, suffering builds a solid tie between islands and the mainland. So it was during the Simba uprising.

The Congolese, both Christian and non-Christian, saw white missionaries suffer in ways they had never known before. They heard the cries of pain from missionaries undergoing cruel beatings, saw the blood and tears. They also observed missionaries' children, of all ages, under severe pressure.

Blood of missionaries and Congolese believers was mingled in martyrdom. Fears and prayers for deliverance were shared in prisons and forest hideouts. In a few weeks, in a way that would have been impossible during years of ordinary living, the common humanity of missionaries and Congolese was demonstrated. The demonstration proved beyond doubt the love of each for the other.

This experience of the fellowship of suffering seems to be behind present repeated insistence on the missionaries' return to the Congo, both by the Congolese church and by the government. And it is also a strong factor in the missionaries' desire to return.

But the bridges of suffering connected with other parts of the mainland as well.

One was the Belgian community, with which the missionaries had negligible dealings during all the prior years of this century. Now, caught in the same mortal storm, each group came to appreciate the other. Planters and missionaries who had never been inside each others' homes now shared the same prison cell and hotel room. A Christian witness was given and Bibles were distributed, in response to requests. And at least one elderly Belgian planter trusted Christ in Hotel Victoria, through the missionaries' witness.

Another bridge — a narrow one — was built between missionaries and American State Department employees. Perhaps more than before, foreign service experts came to understand the part missionaries play in modern international relations. And during the weeks of imprisonment suffered by Michael Hoyt and his aides, Herbert Jenkinson ("Kinso") fulfilled many aspects of consular representation. That he did so with such skill indicates the value of 43 years' service. (The United States government later wrote Mr. Jenkinson a letter expressing its appreciation for his leadership.)

Another bridge connected Protestant missionaries with Roman Catholic priests and nuns — who suffered beyond our understanding. Part of the reason for their great suffering was doubtless the dual role, civil as well as religious, many of them performed during the years of Belgian rule. Another was the mysterious clothing the various orders wore — their religious habits. The Simbas, many of them young boys, were curious about what was beneath large hats and flowing gowns. The mystery of celibacy was still another factor.

In the previous chapter, Margaret Hayes told of the love shown her by nuns and priests in the convent, and later in the forest. "Truly the fellowship of suffering is a very precious fellowship, for it sweeps away all barriers of language, color and creed." This is her comment.

Not that creed was forgotten — Margaret remained a Protestant Christian, aware of the differences. She continued to observe her days of prayer, alone. But creedal differences were no longer an insuperable barrier. In the experience of suffering shared, Jesus Christ became the transcendent fact of belief.

The Congolese pastor (see chapter, "Safari is Sorrow"), speaking to his fellow prisoners who were about to die, emphasized this truth: "Roman Catholic is a name; Protestant is a name; but the One who died on the cross to save us from our sins is the Lord Jesus Christ, whom God the Father gave to redeem us. Trust *Him.*"

Charles Davis mentions the same fellowship of Roman Catholics and Protestants. "The last three weeks we were imprisoned, most of the other prisoners were Catholics. There was a drawing together on the basis of what people really were, rather than the title they bore. Among Protestants, you found that titles such as Presbyterian, Evangelical Covenant, Baptist, Unevangelized Fields Mission, Africa Inland Mission, Independent, all fell away and you got to the core of the matter: was this

person a brother in Christ? And the titles Catholic and Protestant became unimportant in those extreme days.

"You wanted to find out by the testimony a man bore, and
the way he lived, whether he was a son of God through faith
in Christ. A great many barriers were knocked down.

"It was very obvious at Hotel des Chutes and the Victoria
Hotel that fellowship was on the basis of whether a person
expressed Christian love or not. Paul Carlson himself said that
his life was saved a half-dozen times by the love shown to him
by Catholic priests along the route as he made his way into
Stanleyville.

"Love became the important measure of faith in those days,
rather than the title you bore or the religious habit you wore."

But it would not be quite accurate to credit the bridge of
suffering completely for this fresh, living rapport between
Protestants and Roman Catholics during the Congo crisis.
Without doubt, the reconciling influence of Pope John XXIII
and the Vatican Councils were important factors.

Charles Davis recalls how Dr. Paul Carlson was reading Hans
Küng's *Justification* in Hotel Victoria. "He'd been given this
book by a Catholic priest on his way to Stanleyville, while he
was at a Catholic mission station. While he was there, he told
me, he had many discussions with the priests about Christianity and the Bible. The monsignor in charge had given Paul
this book. Paul asked me to read Küng's book, and he wanted
to discuss it with me since I had a background in theology.
We never really had this discussion, because of the rapidity of
events, the tremendous increase in aggression during those last
days. But I read it, and agreed with Paul that there was nothing 'unworthy of Protestantism' in it."

What does Dr. Küng, dean of the theological faculty at
University of Tübingen, West Germany, say in this book that
excited Dr. Carlson's interest? Here is a typical quotation,

which may help to show why fellowship was possible between Protestants and many Catholics during the Simba uprising:

"The deepest reason for the *sola fides* [faith alone] is the *solus Christus* [Christ alone]. It is He alone in whom man is justified and revealed as justified. Faith is faith in *Him*. Faith is justifying insofar as it recognizes and realizes the justification which comes about in Christ as the verdict of God, and insofar as it expects everything from Christ and nothing from itself, everything from grace and nothing from its own thoughts, words, and undertakings. . . .

" '*Sola fides*' makes good sense when it is used to express . . . the total incapacity of man for any kind of self-justification. In justification the sinner can give nothing which he does not receive by God's grace. He stands there with his hands entirely empty. Just as Abraham in Genesis 15:6, and Romans 4:3, and as the Israelites before Moses in Exodus 4:31: 'And the people believed; and when they heard that the Lord had visited the people of Israel and that He had seen their affliction, they bowed their heads and worshiped.' This man is a man who knows that he has nothing to build for God, but he accepts God's word, like David: 'Would you build me a house to dwell in? . . . Moreover the Lord declares to you that the Lord *will make you* a house' (II Samuel 7:5, 11). This man is a man who will not dash off on a charger, but whose power lies in quietness and trust (cf. Isaiah 30:15, 16), who receives the kingdom of God like a little child (Mark 10:15), and who says nothing else than a Marian 'Let it be to me' (Luke 1:38); a man who expects nothing from himself, but expects all from God, who is completely open to that which is his only refuge — this man is the man who does not work but *believes*, and therefore radically excludes any self-boasting."

Suffering has removed the bridges.

White missionaries have bled from the whip, been mutilated, suffered in filthy prisons. Families have been broken — not by the slave trader, who separated husband from wife, parents from children, but by the Simba rifle. And with the same tragic result.

Conscious or unconscious, the thought is there: "We are equal in suffering. White people have accepted the very lowest place. Now we are equal."

19/The Saddest Day

AT SIX-THIRTY TUESDAY MORNING, November 24, Chuck Davis was awakened by the sound of airplanes flying over the city.

From the windows of room 103, he watched the planes — sometimes they came in very low, seeming to buzz the hotel; at other times they flew much higher. He noticed that they seemed to swoop down especially low over in the direction of the airport. Back and forth they flew, small fighter planes, criss-crossing Stanleyville.

Apart from the roar of engines, the city was silent. No gunfire, no rockets.

"Everybody outside! At once, outside!" A Simba ran through the halls screaming his command.

"He sounds excited."

"No wonder. Do you think this is it?"

"I don't know. But if it is, I hope they didn't mean what they said about killing the hostages."

On his way out of the room, Chuck picked up his Bible (which he tucked into his belt in back), and his toothbrush (which went into his hip pocket). He was afraid of what was coming; therefore he told the Lord he was afraid, and asked for strength.

"Run! Get going!" A Simba shouted at the stream of people as they emerged from the building. "That way!" — pointing down the street.

It seemed as if half the prisoners were already running in the direction indicated, toward a concentration of gunfire.

Chuck ran beside Paul Carlson. "What in the world are we doing here?" he asked.

"I don't know, Chuck. Maybe they're planning to use us as a shield to slow up the Belgians."

Up ahead, and about a block away, a machine gun was fired. The prisoners increased their pace, turned at a corner. Davis and Carlson were part of the stream of people who followed.

Armed Simbas halted the hostages on the cross street — a rather narrow one — and ordered them to sit down on the ground. Colonel Opepe was there, a rifle slung over his left shoulder.

This was the first time in several days that the prisoners had seen the colonel; rumor had it that he had deserted to the Nationalist forces with about 50 of his officers. So it was confusing to see him there.

"Haven't I protected you up to this time? Haven't I been your friend? Why are your brothers coming now?" Opepe seemed to take the arrival of rescue forces as a personal affront.

The machine gun was being fired at closer range now: the corner of a building at the end of the block was struck by bullets.

Perhaps the soldier was made nervous by the sound of approaching guns. Whatever the reason, a Simba guard at the rear of the crowd panicked and began to fire his Sten rifle. This was enough to trigger the other guards, who began to shoot into the crowd.

A machine gun on a tripod was pointed directly at the prisoners. But the Simbas' attempts to fire it were unsuccessful; it had jammed. At point-blank range, its effect would have been catastrophic if the Simbas had been able to use it.

The prisoners fell down flat on the street and waited for the bullets to come. This was the end, Chuck Davis thought — his mind raced with the details of how soon, how many bullets, how much damage. He prayed for Muriel, for Beth and Steve.

He was frightened, even though he knew that his future was safe. "I'd be with the Lord, I knew that. But the moment before death is a terrible one to recollect." On his right and on his left, people were hit by bullets.

After what seemed like an endless period of time, the guns were silenced — probably to reload. Al Larson and some of the others took this opportunity to make a dash for safety. Chuck joined them.

Others, including Del Carper, played dead and remained in the street.

Dr. Carlson ran to the right of the house that was nearest, and headed for the back, to the right. Eight or nine, including Al and Chuck, made for a porch at the front of the same house.

The porch had a masonry wall, about five feet off the ground. It was necessary to climb over this wall — the porch steps were at the far side, seemingly in the direct line of fire. Al Larson hesitated only a moment, then went over the wall and kicked open a door into the house. As the prisoners climbed onto the porch, Dr. Carlson ran up from the rear of the house. Perhaps he had seen someone back there, and sought safety at the front.

Paul motioned for Chuck to go over the wall; the others had already entered the house. Chuck dove, hitting his knee and back. Then he turned around to take Paul Carlson's hand, which was outstretched.

But as a gun went off nearby, the doctor fell or jumped from the wall. Chuck ran into the house.

At that moment, Paul Carlson lay dead in the street.

Inside the house, Chuck looked for a place to conceal himself from the Simbas he knew would soon follow. Seeing a closet not far from the entrance to the house, its door ajar, he ran and threw himself into it. There he found seven other men, including Al Larson.

Through the closet's door, glass at the top half, a moment later they saw a man come by with a child. They put the child, an eight-year-old girl, in their midst. They all huddled as close as they could, trying not to disturb the bottles and utensils that were stored inches away. One of the Belgians was frantically viewing an attic entrance ten feet above.

A Simba ran into the house and passed by the closet. Chuck saw him through the glass part of the door. The Simba — by the grace of God, Chuck is certain — didn't notice any of the nine hostages huddled on the floor.

Several moments later, they heard shots from another part of the house. Perhaps the Simba was trying to flush the game. But inside the closet, all were completely quiet.

In the silence, Chuck prayed again for Muriel and their children. Later, thinking back, he was surprised that he didn't pray for himself. But the thought never entered his mind; he prayed rather for Muriel at Kilometer 8, while guns exploded in the house and on the street outside.

The Simba strode past the closet again, this time headed for the porch. He evidently saw nothing beyond the glass door of the closet, nor did he stop to look.

About ten minutes passed.

Then, in English, a voice: "I know they're in here." Chuck recognized the voice of an American who had played dead on the street — could it have been only 15 minutes earlier?

IN BELGIUM after release, Marcel DeBuisson (below with his wife) tells newsman, "I think the one real man I have met in my life was Dr. Paul Carlson." Paratrooper (above) bends over Dr. Carlson's body. *(UPI)*

Dr. Carlson's wife, Lois, and son, Wayne, kneel at casket. Congolese who attended funeral are shown (right).

The American had seen the hostages enter the house. Perhaps they were dead — he'd heard the shooting inside. But he knew they were in there.

Now he opened the closet door, and the occupants untangled themselves and fell out. The American, who was accompanied by two Belgian paratroopers, kept repeating, "It's all right, you're safe. You're safe."

The soldiers repeated the same words in French. Compassion was in their tone and in the expression on their weather-beaten faces.

"You're safe."

But what about the rest? What about Paul Carlson?

Chuck ran to the corner of the porch and looked down. Paul's body was below him, on the ground. Six bullets had entered his body: four, the chest; one, the head; one, the hip.

"I have his Bible," a young Mennonite prisoner said. "He wanted his wife to have it."

(The word "Peace" was written twice in the Bible, alongside dates of the last two days of his life.)

And his body, that fragile earthly dwelling that had been subjected to so much abuse and pain in the past few months, looked peaceful despite its violent end. Seeing the body, Chuck "just cried and cried."

"I remember saying over and over to Al Larson, 'Dead. He's dead.' Al did his best to comfort me, but he was all shook up like the rest of us. You couldn't feel any other way with all that bloodshed and people torn to pieces all around you.

"I must have cried for fifteen minutes. Then I was sitting down on the ground with Dr. Marescotti, in this place where they had taken the bodies. It was sort of a first-aid center. The rescue troops were all around us — they were really guarding us well.

"Then they brought in a man with his throat cut from ear

to ear. The top of his head on the left side had been blown off. Dr. Marescotti and I just sat there in the blood and cried. We just cried. He said, 'What can I do? Under the most perfect conditions I couldn't help this man.'

"So he asked me to pray. I didn't even have the sense to pray, so this Italian doctor who wasn't even a Christian, to whom we'd been witnessing for three weeks, said, 'Pray. We've got to pray over this man.'

"I prayed. I know the man heard me — this living dead person.

"Usually I'm pretty sure of myself. That morning I wasn't sure of anything except that the Lord was the only reason I was there, still alive.

"I thought then," says Chuck Davis, "and again and again during those next few hours, of how I was so close to Paul . . . and that only one of us could have gone over that wall . . . and I might have been the second one.

"Because Paul Carlson died, I live. I figure that this doubles my responsibility as a Christian minister."

U. S. Consul Michael Hoyt
after rescue, with Ambassa-
dor McMurtrie Godley
(left) and vice-consul
David K. Grinwis. *(UPI)*

Italian nuns describe Bafw
sende killings to missionari
Al Larson and Richard Sig
(UPI)

20/Lions Kill a Shepherd

MURIEL AND THE OTHERS at Kilometer 8 were awakened at about six o'clock in the morning by the same planes that brought Chuck out of his bed to the window at Victoria Hotel.

Everyone, including the children, ran outside to stare up at the planes. Then they went back in for breakfast.

Someone turned on B.B.C. radio, which warned of a serious attack on Stanleyville that day.

Breakfast over, Bible reading and prayer followed as usual. Just as the praying began, Muriel looked outside, then said to Ione McMillan, "Uh-oh, there come two of them." Two Simbas walked up the path toward the house, without a car.

Standard procedure in previous weeks — so the women wouldn't be involved — was for the men to go outside to deal with the Simbas. The women kept out of sight, with the children.

But today was different. The gun-carrying Simbas pushed past the men and came bursting into the house. As the women and children drew back in surprise and fright, the Simbas turned the breakfast tables upside down. Plates and utensils went crashing to the floor, while food spilled in all directions.

Next the Simbas began an erratic, wild search of the room and its contents. One item they found was a slide projector, with which they were unfamiliar.

"Radio transmitter!" one shouted accusingly.

Finding a bag packed by one missionary for possible flight, they dumped its contents on the floor and filled it with food, mostly canned goods.

Then they ordered the quiet group of people to go outside and line up. Muriel, carrying Beth, was the last one through the door.

"They gave me a push down the steps and I fell down. I'll never forget it — Mrs. McMillan was just infuriated that they would push me when I had a child in my arms. So she turned right around at gunpoint (she might have been killed any moment) and came back to help me up."

Outside, the Simbas lined the women up, making the men stand off to the side.

One of the Simbas pointed to a motor which was used to draw water: "We heard that and thought it was a plane." But the motor hadn't been turned on until after the planes disappeared, and his lie seemed transparent to the missionaries. The Simbas had come to get the white people at Kilometer 8, not to investigate the sound of a plane.

"Get back in the house," they told the women and children. They ordered the two men — Hector McMillan and Bob McAllister — to remain outside.

In the living room, the women and children sat in a silent circle. The Simba who had accompanied them back into the house "screamed at us like a madman." Then he turned to go outside again. But instead, he turned around at the door and shot around the room ten or twelve times.

"We had discussed this before, that if something like this

happened, we should all dive to the floor," Muriel recalls. "But somehow, when it happens, you just don't have sense enough to get down. Instead, you sit there looking at his eyes as he shoots around the room. You don't know what to do.

"But finally we all got down, trying to shield the children. One of the older missionaries started to quote the 46th Psalm. It was a real comfort to us . . ."

God is our refuge and strength, a very present help in trouble.

Therefore will not we fear, though the earth be removed, and though the mountains be carried into the midst of the sea;

Though the waters thereof roar and be troubled, though the mountains shake with the swelling thereof. Selah.

There is a river, the streams whereof shall make glad the city of God, the holy place of the tabernacles of the most High.

God is in the midst of her; she shall not be moved: God shall help her, and that right early.

The heathen raged, the kingdoms were moved: he uttered his voice, the earth melted.

The Lord of hosts is with us; the God of Jacob is our refuge. Selah.

Come, behold the works of the Lord, what desolations he hath made in the earth.

He maketh wars to cease unto the end of the earth; he breaketh the bow, and cutteth the spear in sunder; he burneth the chariot in the fire.

Be still, and know that I am God: I will be exalted among the heathen, I will be exalted in the earth.

The Lord of hosts is with us; the God of Jacob is our refuge. Selah.

"Of course, we were all praying out loud. The two oldest McMillan boys — Ken and Paul — were the only ones injured by the Simba's shots; we were so thankful their injuries weren't serious.

"The younger children were crying, although Beth and Steve never did cry. They just lay still on the floor, and whenever anyone raised his head to look around, Steve would say, 'Put your head down! Put your head down!' He was just so scared that the Lions would come back.

"And then we heard some shots outside. We didn't know anything about what was going on out there — where the Lions were, or what had happened to Hector McMillan and Bob McAllister.

"Finally, the two wives said they just had to go out to check on their husbands. They just couldn't stand it any longer. First they looked out the window, and they didn't see any Lions. So they went outside, followed by the rest of us.

"There we found Hector McMillan, who had been killed instantly. And Bob McAllister, who was getting up from the ground."

Bob explained what had happened.

"I heard them shoot, and turned around. There was Hector on the ground. 'You shot my friend,' I told them. Then this one Simba shot at me. I'll always believe that the Lord knocked me down, because that Lion really believed he'd killed me, too."

Bob and some of the women carried Hector McMillan's body into the living room, where they gently laid it down. When they had cleaned it up, Ione McMillan called her six sons — aged ten to seventeen — back into the house.

"Your father has gone to be with the Lord, and I want you to see him before his body gets cold."

As the boys filed into the living room, most of the others left for another part of the house, where they prayed. Several stayed with Ione and her sons; they too had a time of prayer.

Bob McAllister hunted for a box to put the beloved Hector's

body in. If Hector had been there, he'd have put one together in a jiffy.

Where had the Lions gone? When would they return, perhaps with reinforcements, to complete the massacre?

Nobody knew. The silence outside the house was ominous.

Some of the women, including Muriel, felt that they should go into the forest a little way, in case the Lions should return. Bob didn't know what to advise. He reminded them that the forest was dark and damp and dangerous. There'd be no place to sleep at night. And they'd have to take food. But it was up to each woman to decide.

If there were an African to lead them, it would be different. But all who lived on the mission property had fled deep into the forest. There wasn't anyone around, except the Lions.

So Bob left it up to each woman to decide what the Lord wanted her to do.

Twelve, including most of the children, went into the forest. The other 12 stayed at the mission station, partly to care for the injured McMillan boys.

The Lord of hosts is with us; the God of Jacob is our refuge.

21/Into the Congo Forest

Ninety years ago, David Livingstone described a Congo forest: "The sun, though directly overhead, cannot penetrate this primeval forest except by sending down at midday a thin pencil of rays into the gloom. The rainwater stands for months in stagnant pools. Climbing plants, from the size of a whipcord to that of a man-of-war hawser, are so numerous that the ancient path is the only passage. When one of the giant trees falls across the path, it forms a breast-high wall to be climbed over, and the mass of tangled plants brought down with the tree makes cutting a path around it a work of time that travelers never undertake."

Undergrowth rises to a height of 15 feet above the ground, while many trees stand 150 to 200 feet high.

Leopards are found in the forest, with apes and many kinds of monkeys. Pythons, cobras, vipers and various other deadly snakes abound. Wolves, jackals and wild hogs are found in the forest. The density of all kinds of insects is beyond imagination.

Into the forbidding Congo forest behind Kilometer 8 mission

station went Muriel Davis and several other women, with the younger children. They also took ten-year-old Marilyn Carper —"We didn't like to have a young girl at the station with the Lions around."

No African was there to guide them; all had fled deep into the forest. So the women and children went alone.

They hurried down a narrow path made by the Africans, hemmed in by dense undergrowth. Not wanting to get too far from the 12 others they'd left at Kilometer 8, they turned into the growth to the left. When all were sitting on the ground, they warned the children to be quiet while they waited. Minutes passed; the little ones were surprisingly quiet.

Fearful of being found in the clearing by Simba pursuers, the women took branches and patched them together to hide their little party from sight. The camouflage was pitifully inadequate, and would doubtless have failed to conceal them from a Simba search party. But they felt safer, hiding under the branches with their children.

And besides, there was nothing else they could do but wait, and try to conceal themselves. The forest was too dense for white people, unaccustomed to jungle travel, to get very far — especially with children.

So they settled down to wait.

"What time is it, Muriel?"

"Twenty to twelve. It seems much later."

"I know. The children are being quiet, aren't they?" The women talked in whispers.

"Yes. I wonder what they're thinking, after all they saw this morning."

Suddenly the silence was broken by a sharp volley of shots, followed by heavy shooting such as the women had never heard before.

Just as suddenly as it had begun, the shooting stopped.

"Jean, do you suppose we'll ever see them again? The Simbas must have returned and killed everyone. And here we are in the forest, with the children."

"Shhh . . . Children, stay right where you are. The Lord Jesus will take care of us."

Only the hum of insects disturbed the heavy silence.

"Muriel, did you hear that?"

"Yes, I think someone's calling. Children, be quiet, just as quiet as you can possibly be."

"Muriel, it's Al. Al's calling me." Jean's voice rose.

"It can't be, Jean. Al's in Stan. Don't start imagining things. And keep your voice down."

"But it *is* Al. Listen."

The voice was louder. "Come on out. Jean, the rest of you, come out of the forest. You're safe. This is Al."

Branches were thrown aside as women and children scrambled out of their tiny place of refuge, back on the path. Al Larson met them while they were still in the forest. Del Carper was with him.

"Where's Chuck?" Muriel was almost afraid to ask. The strain of weeks was in her voice.

"Chuck's all right. He's back in Stan. Or by now I guess he's on his way to Leopoldville. Only two of us could come out here. So the soldiers brought Del and me, to get everyone here at Kilometer 8. You'll see Chuck soon. Now we'll have to hurry — no time to pick up anything. We'll have to get moving right away."

"What was all the shooting?"

"The mercenaries had to shoot their way in here, past the Simbas. We'll probably have to shoot our way back out. Come on, everybody. Hurry! Get in the truck there."

"I'd like to go to the Hangar and get our passports," Muriel said.

"Okay, but make it snappy. Into the truck, everybody. Here, let us help you up."

Muriel ran to her room and got the passports. She also picked up her Bible. It was all anyone took out of Kilometer 8. With Beth, she rode in the truck. Steve was in a jeep.

Hector McMillan's body was left there, unburied. "Some day," he'd once said, "I'm going to give this old body, with all its troubles and limitations, back to the elements. Then I'm going to claim a new body from the Lord."

As the truck rolled down the road, the mercenaries kept up a steady volley of shots into the bush. Later that day they learned that a delay of only 20 minutes would have prevented their escape: a heavy concentration of Simbas in the area sealed off the road at that time. But the margin of safety, though narrow, was enough.

When they reached Stanleyville airport, the little party of 24 from Kilometer 8 joined a stream of refugees — some of them on stretchers — for the mercy airlift to Leopoldville.

Meanwhile, at Leopoldville airport, Chuck Davis had been anxiously waiting for the missionaries from Kilometer 8 to arrive — especially three members of the group. By four o'clock in the afternoon, his tension had built up to a peak. Increasing crowds of government officials, newsmen, photographers and relatives jammed the airport building. When the next plane arrived, the crowd was so dense that Chuck could not get near it.

Suddenly he caught a glimpse of Muriel. But the crowds going in different directions pressed them past each other.

"Merle!"

A few seconds later they were together. "Where are the children?" He dreaded her reply.

"They're okay, both of them. Another missionary has Beth.

Wounded refugees from Stanleyville are carried from plane at Leopoldville (above). Congo President Joseph Kasavubu (below, with aides) shows concern for arriving refugees. (UPI)

A NIGHTMARE ENDS as Beth Davis is carried in the strong arms of a Belgian paratrooper. Beth's parents and other missionaries say that it was the assurance that "Underneath are the everlasting arms" that brought them through the nightmare. (*Paris Match*)

She's up ahead. And I left Steve at the airline counter. But they're perfectly all right."

"Thank God!" And they embraced.

"But dear Hector was killed. We had to leave him — his body — back at Kilometer 8."

"Poor Ione and their boys. Paul Carlson was killed, too. In fact, if he hadn't been — "

"Daddy!"

The next day, Wednesday, in Leopoldville, a prayer meeting was held. In addition to the missionaries who had been rescued, Ralph B. Odman, general director for North America of the Unevangelized Fields Mission, and Homer Dowdy, Michigan Christian newsman, were present. They had just flown to the Congo from the United States.

A missionary who had been rescued the day before began to pray. But after a few words, his voice broke, and he was unable to continue.

"One of us should have picked right up," Chuck Davis says. "But we didn't — not before Ione McMillan."

"Here she had just lost her husband the day before. She faced the responsibility of raising six boys without a father. Yet she was the one who picked right up and prayed by name for every other missionary who was still in the Congo, unaccounted for.

"These are her words: 'I know that You love me, God, and that Hector died in Your will.' "

On Thanksgiving Day 1964, the following day, Charles and Muriel Davis were winging their way back to the United States, to a quiet little town in the hills of western Virginia.

22/Some Congolese Insights

WHAT DO CONGOLESE say about events of recent years in their country? To understand the past and anticipate the future, the answer to this question is important.

To find out, the writer interviewed two responsible pastors, leaders of their churches in the Congo, through interpreters. (Languages: French and Swahili.) Main opinions are reported below, without critical comment.

Assani Benedict, Bo Martin's twin brother, is one of the Congo's outstanding pastors. He shared leadership with Yonama Angondia in the trek from Oicha to Uganda, described in the chapter, "Modern Moses." Church leaders recently set him apart as minister-at-large to the churches in the Congo.

Daniel Makasi is a Baptist pastor in Congo's Kivu province. He is general secretary of the Baptist Association of the Kivu, which has 45 organized churches with 9,000 members.

Assani explains the Simbas' enmity toward the Church in the following dialogue:

The Simbas said to the Church in Congo: "You must stand with us and support our movement."

The Church replied: "We cannot stand with you in a war to kill people. We refuse to participate in your acts of terrorism."

The Simbas said: "Christ didn't die for black people — He died for white people. Therefore you ought to leave the Christian Church. It's only for whites."

The Church replied: "The Word of God says Christ died for everyone, black and white. The Church stands on the Word of God."

The Simbas said: "Don't believe the word of missionaries. They have come here to deceive you."

The Church replied: "Missionaries do not deceive us. They came to tell us of Christ. Our faith is not in the missionaries, but in Christ."

The Simbas said: "If we allow pastors and Christians to continue to pray, we won't win. This is so because you're praying for Tshombe and the national government. Because you do not pray for us to win, you are our enemies." (Many sources mention the Simbas' fear of the prayers of Christians.)

When Christians refused to support them, according to Assani, the Simbas warred against the Church.

Daniel Makasi says that the trouble actually began four years before the Simba uprising, when Patrice Lumumba had just taken office as the Congo's first prime minister.

In the wake of independence and the new nationalism, some Christians, according to Daniel, urged the Baptist Church in Kivu not to work with the missionaries (of Conservative Baptist Foreign Mission Society) any longer. This caused division in the Church. The opposition group, of which Daniel was leader, wanted to continue to support the missionaries at any cost — "They are our fathers in the faith."

The anti-missionary party was able to swing a majority of the Christians to their position, and they formed a purely

African Baptist synod, which excluded all missionaries. Today the synod group continues its independent existence, with 15,000 members.

Both Assani Benedict and Daniel Makasi stress Communist influence on Congolese affairs since 1960. Immediately after independence, they say, Russian Communists were responsible for arousing the Congolese. Later, at the time of the Simba uprising in 1964, it was the Chinese Communists who incited the Congolese to rebellion. Daniel says that 400 Communist agitators, trained by the Chinese, worked in Congo plantations and shops.

How do Congolese Christians explain the cruel, demonic acts of the Simbas?

In the first place, according to Assani, actions of the Simbas did not represent a revival of tribal practices. This was, he emphasizes, a new thing. The impetus came, he believes, from outside the Congo — from Chinese Communists in Tanzania (formerly Tanganyika) and Brazzaville. Prior to their open rebellion, Simba leaders received training there, Assani says, and were told to go back to the Congo and kill their enemies. (Other observers pinpoint Burundi and the Sudan as centers of Communist operations, rather than Tanzania and Brazzaville.)

"You want to rule the Congo," the Chinese Communists told the Simbas, according to Assani, "so you'll have to kill people. We'll help you on one condition: you must get rid of all the white people in the Congo. Get them all out, or kill them, including the missionaries."

The Simbas' hatred was particularly directed toward Congolese pastors and the Church. Many Christians had no connection with the Church; the Simbas' ruthless acts were not against these "loners" so much as against those who stood with the Church.

The Congolese Church maintained a united front against the Simbas with one exception, according to Assani. "Backsliders who were under discipline of the Church tended to join with the Simbas in accusing Christians. Pagans also accused Christians to the Simbas."

A second explanation for the cruelty was the extreme youth of many Simbas. The soldiers were as young as ten years of age; most were between 15 and 18. A few were 20. Officers were older — in their twenties or early thirties.

A third factor in explaining the Simbas' cruel, often senseless deeds, according to Assani, was the heavy drinking and hemp-smoking (a narcotic). Missionaries have mentioned the drunken, erratic behavior of many Simbas.

How many Congolese Christians were killed by the Simbas? A general estimate is 10,000, which includes many children. The total number of Congolese killed is in the hundreds of thousands.

What are the effects of this suffering? Assani Benedict and Daniel Makasi mention the following:

(1) The great trouble caused Christians to stand fast in Jesus Christ. The Church stood strong, and today it continues to stand strong.

(2) Many people who did not come to church services before come now. Backsliders have repented and returned. "Now everyone sees that the Simbas tried to wipe out the Church," Assani says, "but they were not able. God is in the Church. The heathen are saying that they want to join up with us. 'Because of you,' they say, 'the Congo is saved.' For the first time, many heathen are interested in the Gospel."

Daniel adds that their great suffering opened the eyes of many heathen Congolese to the fact that they need the Gospel.

(3) The great wave of persecution and suffering brought a new sense of oneness to the Christians.

(4) More than before, the Congo realizes it needs missionaries. Surprisingly, both Assani and Daniel consider this a day of great opportunity for missionaries. "The Kivu parliament recently affirmed by vote that they welcome back to the Congo all missionaries who are willing to come and work and suffer with us," says Daniel. "The number of Christian believers has doubled since 1960, and we can expect much more growth. But we need missionaries."

What kind of missionaries are needed?

"Technicians" is the word Daniel uses to explain what the Congo — and in his opinion, all of Africa — wants. "Not American pastors or evangelists, but technicians who can train our men to be pastors and evangelists and teachers. We need men who will show us how to plant churches, and help them grow. These technicians must teach us doctrine and Bible and how to serve the Church."

Medical doctors are also needed in great numbers.

"And professors to teach our young people. We need Christian educators who can prepare leaders for the Church from the new generation. We need a new university which will be completely Christian."

(5) Another result of the Simba uprising that Daniel has observed is a new respect for missionaries and their opinions by American State Department personnel in the Congo. Consular staff members found during the months of 1964 that American missionaries understood the situation in depth, and reacted with sense and bravery.

In spite of their optimism, Assani and Daniel are realistic.

"Let us not forget this time of sorrow," Assani says. "Let us not forget what the Lord has brought us through. And let us be prepared for what may come in the future."

"Yes," agrees Daniel. "The days may be few. Let us stand together and do the work while there is time. Africa is in the midst of great danger."

"After these times of suffering, I have a stronger desire to serve God than ever before." Assani speaks intensely. "My heart is surging with much more joy than before this time of sorrow.

"But Christians in America should be prepared for this, too. Our word from the Church in the Congo to the Church in America is Romans 8:35 to the end of the chapter."

Who shall separate us from the love of Christ? Shall tribulation, or distress, or persecution, or famine, or nakedness, or peril, or sword? As it is written, "For thy sake we are being killed all the day long; we are regarded as sheep to be slaughtered."

No, in all these things we are more than conquerors through him who loved us. For I am sure that neither death, nor life, nor angels, nor principalities, nor things present, nor things to come, nor powers, nor height, nor depth, nor anything else in all creation, will be able to separate us from the love of God in Christ Jesus our Lord. (RSV)

23/What Is a Martyr?

mar • tyr, fr. Gr. *martyr-*, lit., witness: one who
voluntarily suffers death as the penalty of witnessing to and refusing to renounce his religion
. . . (*Webster's Seventh New Collegiate Dic-
tionary*)

LIKE EVERYTHING ELSE in the twentieth century, martyrdom
is no longer a simple concept.

Gone is the either-or alternative, "Recant or perish" of first-
century Rome, the Inquisition, Bloody Queen Mary. In its
place is a complex of primitive cultural terror . . . racial hatred
. . . political pressure . . . Communist expansion.

Countless men and women "of whom the world was not
worthy" have laid down their lives for Christ in this century.
But the motivation of their killers has more often than not
been rooted in anti-white, anti-West, anti-civilization emo-
tions, rather than in anti-Christianity.

What is a martyr?

In the early years of the Christian Church, and in some
parts of the world today, the answer to that question seems
easy. A martyr is "one who voluntarily suffers death as the
penalty of witnessing to and refusing to renounce his religion."

But the outstanding example of martyrdom in our times, that of the five noble young men who were killed by Auca Indians in Ecuador, does not fit the classic definition. Jim Elliot, Nate Saint, *et al.* died at the hands of savages without opportunity to witness to their religion or renounce it. Their killers' motivation would have been similar toward representatives of Shell Oil or Coca-Cola. The Aucas considered strangers — engineers or anthropologists or missionaries — a threat; therefore they killed them.

And in the Congo, why were Paul Carlson, Hector McMillan, Bill McChesney, Chester Burk, and scores of other missionaries martyred? For their Christian witness, their refusal to renounce what they believed and taught? If that was so, how do we explain the fact that the Rebels largely passed over British nationals in the beginning? And were Belgian planters, who made little claim to religious belief, also martyrs because bullets from the same guns shot them?

We are forced to conclude that general missionary identification with the policies and practices of their home countries had more to do with the murder of Dr. Paul Carlson and the others than their identification with Jesus Christ and His missionary program. This sort of national identification is unavoidable: skin color is white, and nationality is American (or British or German), without regard to results in time of crisis.

In addition, whether they like it or not, today's missionaries carry the heavy baggage of history. This factor in persecution and martyrdom may not be as easy to document as United States aid to the Tshombe government, but it is present. Leopold's ghost follows the Belgians as old slave ships follow the Americans. And subsidies and special privileges under a colonial government are not forgotten when independence comes.

But why were Jim Elliot and his friends exposed to danger on that Curaray River sandbar? What explains Hector McMillan's presence at Kilometer 8 in the heat of a Rebel uprising?

Here we come to the factor that seems to distinguish martyrdom for Jesus Christ from dying in the line of anthropological research or business affairs: motivation.

Motivation of the killed, not the killer, is the key to martyrdom. And this is the common element in martyrdom, regardless of the century or country or culture.

Paul Carlson and Hector McMillan were in the Congo for the purpose of a Christian witness. They were exposed to danger because they chose to be in a dangerous place for Jesus Christ.

A martyr, then, is a man or woman who, with faith in Jesus Christ according to the Scriptures, for a purpose he conceives to be his Christian duty (usually, but not invariably, a Christian witness), knowingly exposes himself to danger with the possibility of death, and dies. The killers may or may not have religious or anti-Christian motivation, but the result of the martyr's death is a Christian witness.

It should perhaps be noted that, according to Christian doctrine, God's adversary, Satan, is the ultimate reason for the persecution and martyrdom of Christian witnesses. St. Paul has explained this: "For we are not contending against flesh and blood, but against the principalities, against the powers, against the world rulers of this present darkness, against the spiritual hosts of wickedness in the heavenly places" (Ephesians 6:12, RSV).

If this is so, the motivation of the killers is less important. Something deeper and more significant than primitive fear or anti-white hatred or any other reason for killing is in control.

Martyrdom has always been considered the crown of Christian experience. Martin Luther wrote with a touch of regret: "I was not worthy to shed my blood for Christ, as many of my fellow confessors of the Gospel have done. Yet this honor was also denied to the beloved disciple, John the Evangelist."

But in our times, the effect of martyrdom upon the Christian community seems to have become even deeper. Who can estimate the number of missionaries who trace their call to the murder of John and Betty Stam in China during the 'thirties, the Auca killings in the late 'fifties? And a similar strong effect in the Church, especially among young people, is resulting from the Congo murders.

Perhaps there is reaction in this — reaction to the softness of American life, to the "goof-off age," to the absence of ideals and commitment to a cause.

Here were people who were so committed to Jesus Christ that they died for Him. And they died bravely.

*   *   *

Let dissolution come when it will, it can do the Christian no harm, for it will be but a passage out of a prison into a palace; out of a sea of troubles into a haven of rest; out of a crowd of enemies into an innumerable company of true, loving and faithful friends; out of shame, reproach and contempt into exceeding great and eternal glory.

JOHN BUNYAN

24/"I Will Build My Church"

WESTERN COLONIALISM has ended. This event in our generation is so basic that it must have sweeping consequences for all movements and activities which were carried on before independence, and continue to exist. And missionary work is in the forefront of such activities.

Political instability in the new nations, and current educational and material lacks are misleading. This is dangerous, for if we are deluded into believing that these factors mean "business as usual" after things have quieted down, we shall not make the radical adjustments necessary in the new environment.

Unfortunately, the greater the instability and deprivations of new nations, the more their leaders tend to suspect the former powers of continued colonial ambitions. This suspicion is real, though it may be groundless, and affects all types of work that depend upon cooperation.

Another related fear of the new nations is that economic independence may not follow political freedom. Even if the former powers have no continuing colonial designs on the new nation, leaders reason, they probably will do all they can to preserve economic dependency. This sort of half-freedom was not in the planning of the architects of independence.

Because of these fears, and their desire to consolidate an image of independence as quickly as possible, new nations are often vulnerable to the appeal of world communism. Or they may adopt a posture of neutralism for the same reasons. In either event, results are similar for the West and its missionaries.

For its part, world communism is eager to exploit political instability, distrust of the Western powers, and material and educational deprivations, wherever they are found. And communism has developed techniques for such exploitation. The Congo was an example of these techniques at work.

Much as it might help, missionaries cannot change their white skin or their Western nationality. They are therefore objects of suspicion and persecution whenever fresh trouble develops.

Missionaries who are returning to the Congo today, even more than those who returned after the independence trouble of 1960, must reckon the possible cost. These are men and women who know what a day might bring, and are willing to face it for the sake of Jesus Christ and Congolese for whom He died and lives.

To the extent possible within this framework of suspicion, and without disloyalty to the country of his citizenship, today's missionary must be supranational; he must stand apart from his own country's policies.

Of more importance is the missionary's own attitude toward his brethren, especially colleagues, in the national church. This may not be a life-protector if trouble develops, but it is a church-builder. And in view of the always possible and imminent exclusion of missionaries from various nations, church-building has a prime place in all missionary work today.

Today's missionary in the Congo and other nations has more problems, or fewer advantages in comparison with the past.

The West is not respected in missionary lands as it once was. Two world wars and several lesser wars, racial incidents, publicity about our other problems, and Communist propaganda have damaged our "Christian" image. The American missionary, therefore, is denied the respect and deference accorded prior generations of missionaries.

He must build his own image in a changed and suspicious environment. And an image that developed during nearly a century of existence under the aegis of colonial powers will not be changed overnight.

Missionaries in the Congo have been among Africa's finest. Screening of candidates for this field by sending agencies, both Protestant and Roman Catholic, has been unusually careful. The country's dire need of social and educational advance in this century probably stimulated a demand for excellence.

As a result, the men and women who went to the Congo were competent, well-trained and stable. Their magnificence in the face of crisis represented the sort of people they had been in peaceful times.

Was the Congo crisis a judgment on missionary work in that country? Nothing could be further from the truth. As indicated throughout this book, missionaries in the Congo were unusually responsive to changing patterns in the culture and the Holy Spirit's work in the Church. Hector McMillan, Mary Baker, Margaret Hayes, Paul Carlson: these people loved the Congolese, not with white paternalism, but as brothers. They were servants of the Church in Congo for Jesus' sake. And they were typical of the missionary force.

The same can be said of Bo Martin and Assani Benedict, Daniel Makasi and Yonama Angondia. They loved the missionaries as brothers; they were willing to risk life itself for these white men and women from overseas.

Why, then, has the Church in Congo suffered so?

"Whom the Lord loveth, He chasteneth." In the mystery of this statement is the key to why Congolese Christians and missionaries have suffered so deeply since independence, particularly during the Simba uprising.

Among Protestant missionaries, one observer comments, the spirit of oneness in the Congo is only matched by that of the missionary force in India. When missionaries from different societies were thrown together in prison, at Kilometer 8, or elsewhere, they already knew each other and had spiritual respect for one another. In most instances they had previously cooperated in LECO or some other field project.

LECO (*Librairie Evangelique au Congo* — in French, *librairie* means both bookstore and publishing house) is an outstanding example of the results of cooperation among missionary societies in a particular country. In 1946 the Leopoldville Bookshop was reorganized as LECO. Fourteen missions and two Bible societies subscribed funds, property was secured, a printing press was installed, and in 1948 production began. The literature needs of many different Congolese languages have been met through LECO, and many millions of book pages have been printed. This inter-society agency continues to serve a wide spectrum of missions with evangelical materials.

When you talk to survivors of the Simba uprising, you notice that a martyr complex is singularly absent. These men and women have no bitterness; in almost every instance — including widows — they are anxious to return to the Congo and their former fields of service. Hector McMillan's oldest son, Ken, hopes to return, perhaps as a medical missionary.

The attitude of these missionaries tends to be one of self-examination. They ask such questions as, "Have we, over the years, made the Gospel so relevant to the lives of Africans that they could see it?" "Was our message related to the culture and life of these people in such a way that they could find the freedom that is in Christ?"

When these missionaries were isolated from their home churches, their home boards, and even from their home governments by the Simba uprising, they did not panic. Men such as Al Larson took the full weight of leadership that the situation required.

During those months, missionaries made decisions that were far-reaching, both in terms of personal safety and — of even greater importance — the future of missions in the Congo. Some of these decisions affected the course of international relations.

In a few instances, home churches and well-meaning pastors and other leaders in America wrote letters to missionaries, telling them, from several thousand miles' safe distance, what to do.

"Those letters potentially were a threat to my life," says one Congo missionary. "If my mail had been opened in those days, I could have been accused and executed as an American government agent, getting my instructions from overseas."

A rule that should be impressed on the church and its leaders is this: In any time of crisis, when missionaries are in a hot spot, limit communications to words of spiritual encouragement. Don't try to tell them what to do. Pray for them and trust them to make the right decisions. They know much more about the situation than people at home can possibly know. Sometimes they know more than the State Department or Foreign Office.

And if we depend upon the mature leadership and decision-making of our missionaries in times of crisis, what of other, ordinary times?

Here we face one of the great problems of missionaries in the Congo and in many other parts of the world today: Pressure on them to carry out the dictates of their home churches, pastors and other Christian leaders who are removed from the actual situation on the field.

Some churches demand that their missionaries carry the burden of American organization wherever they go in the world. They are expected to build a church in the American image, patterned after a particular type of American ecclesiastical conscience — not a church based on the situation in Congo or somewhere else. Leverage to accomplish this control is usually financial, expressed or implied.

The basic question that the missionary must decide, in the face of such pressures, is whether cooperation in the work of planting the Church in the Congo should be based on organizational affiliations, or on personal, living fellowship with Christ, the Head of the Church. To most, the answer seems obvious from the Scriptures.

Meanwhile, most Congolese Christians who are aware of the pressures from abroad are inclined to reject every attempt to impose ecclesiastical colonialism on them. They want a Congolese church, not a carbon copy of the church in America or somewhere else. This inner Christian drive to build their own church meshes with external nationalistic forces; the result is resistance to the imposition of organization patterns from the outside.

Difficult as it may be, the churches in England, the United States and Canada must trust the Holy Spirit to build the Church in Congo. And it will not be surprising if His building does not correspond in all details to the overseas pattern.

The Congo crisis is the crisis of missions. In a broader sense, it is the crisis of the church throughout the world, including Communist-controlled nations and the West.

In recent decades, the church has lost its leverage on governments, not merely in the new nations, but throughout the world. This is true of missions in the Congo, with the end of Belgian colonial rule. It is also true of China and North Korea, Eastern Europe, and other Communist-controlled countries. And it is true of the "post-Christian" West, where the prevailing climate is more of neutralism at best, atheism at worst, than of pro-Christianity.

In such times, it is not surprising that a ghetto-like psychology has overtaken the Church. The minority movement, without leverage, easily becomes defensive, facing inward rather than outward. Security is found in close association with others of like opinions, without the danger or tension of confrontation with opposing views.

We must all be reminded today, wherever the Church is, that our situation is not unlike that of first century Christians. They had no leverage through government favor, no security through popular acceptance. Yet those Christians "turned the world upside down."

Several years ago, Dr. Ferenc Kiss, chairman of a department in the University of Budapest (Hungary) Medical School, gave the following analysis of the Church in a Communist society:

"The inner natures of communism and Christianity are completely opposed. Communism is materialistic; Christianity is spiritual. Communism denies God and the revelation He has given of Himself; Christianity proclaims both. Communism is the imposition of socialism on the masses by the force of dictatorship; Christianity is an individual conviction not by force but by love, and Christianity results in unselfish love for others.

"Communism aims to give material salvation to men on earth by force; Christianity gives spiritual salvation from heaven by faith. Christianity solves the problem between man and man on the principle of the love of God.

"It is well-known that communism has attempted to destroy Christianity by persecution, but it did not and it cannot succeed.

"What is the position of Christianity in communist countries today, almost a half century after the Russian Revolution of 1917?

"In the battle with communism, the large established churches lost three things, as follows: (1) Large and small properties; (2) Influence in the State; (3) The majority of their nominal members.

"Communism argues that neither Jesus nor His Apostles had property in the State, and their followers were not nominal Christians. Communism says Christians must be satisfied with apostolic principles. In effect, communism forces Christianity to return to simple Biblical principles.

"In Communist countries, the evangelical Christian still retains today his three great treasures: (1) The Bible as the Word of God and final authority; (2) The power of faith and prayer instead of the power of the State; (3) The spiritual fellowship of Christians instead of nominal church or party membership.

"These three treasures neither communism nor any other worldly power can take from evangelical Christians, either by persecutions or by any other means.

"A leader of the anti-God movement put it this way: 'We can change all ideologies and thoughts of men, except the hidden Christ in man.'"

(The medical professor who wrote these words has stood up to repeated tests, both under Nazi and Communist rule. On a number of occasions he has risked his own safety and freedom to protest discrimination toward Jews.)

Dr. Kiss's words are relevant to the Church in the Congo; they are also increasingly relevant to the Church in the West.

When the Church loses its influence on the state, when education becomes an arm of the state rather than of the Church, reality of another kind must come to the front if the Church is to continue to grow.

That reality is, ultimately, "the hidden Christ in man" which shines in a darkening world. Christian character — love, chastity, integrity, courage — won first century Romans and Greeks when the Church had no political influence. And Christian character is the key to growth in the new Congo . . . and the new America.

But Christian character is not displayed in the ghetto; it clashes with the forces of darkness. Pietism in the Christian community is important, but it gives little light beyond.

Men with the prophetic gift are needed in today's Church, men who will awaken a deaf world to moral responsibility and the judgment of God. Such men will exalt God and His Word, they will be men of Christian character, and they will hold life lightly.

Christianity is most exalted in such men, not in institutions. Institutions may be closed. But God's prophets can be heard even in prison, and they shout in death. Witness Paul Carlson, Hector McMillan, the Auca Five, and John and Betty Stam.

But the need is not merely, not even primarily, for prophetic missionaries. Prophetic nationals must also be prepared to suffer in the evil day.

During the Congo uprising, foreign missionaries understandably encouraged their Congolese brethren to flee before the Rebel attackers, thus avoiding suffering and death. In a situation of this kind, any Christian would reason, it's bad enough for the missionaries to be persecuted, without involving the national Church.

But the question arises, as it does when we consider the Com-

munist takeover in China fifteen years earlier: Should missionaries try to shield national Christians from involvement?

A consideration of the Congo crisis provides a positive rather
than negative occasion for such a question, for the courage and
sacrifice of many Congolese Christians in the face of persecution and death (described elsewhere in this book) was a glori-
ous part of this recent incident in church history.

To the writer, at least, it seems that in the new period of
Christian missions, based upon partnership rather than paternalism, the missionary and the national Christians must stand
together when persecution comes.

The missionary should be able to expect support of every
kind from the national Church. If he is accused of preaching
a religion contrary to the nation's interest, prophetic national
leaders should not flee, but stand with him, declaring, "We also
believe and preach this same Christ."

If the missionary is accused as an "economic imperialist," or
an agent advancing his own government's interests, prophetic
national leaders should deny this, affirming his sole religious
activity.

Paternalism sends the children away when trouble comes.
Partnership means standing together. As the Congo incident
showed, partnership may mean suffering and dying together.

In a sense, the change in missions today is the change from
Jesus' "Let these go their way," when He was taken in the
Garden, to "the fellowship of His sufferings" in martyrdom
after Pentecost.

It is both Christian and wise to expect prophetic nationals
to close in around the missionary, and stand with him when
trouble comes. Christian, because it was Christ in Paul Carlson
who led him to lay down his life for his Congolese friends
and patients. The same Christ will lead Congolese to lay down

their lives for white missionaries. Otherwise we are encouraging white heroes, not Christian martyrs.

And wise, because if the foreign missionary stands alone in the face of false accusations, and his missionary activity is tied to Western politics, the work of Jesus Christ will suffer a serious setback when the missionary is martyred or expelled from the country. The silence of national Christians will be interpreted as assent to the charge against the missionary and against Christianity. The brand of "Western, white religion" will stick.

Is it right and fair for the missionary to expect national Christian leaders to stand with him, and be identified with him, in the face of possible death? No, perhaps not. But it is right for him to expect them to join him in a united stand for Jesus Christ. And this is the real meaning of the new partnership in foreign missions.

Today nationals are taking over control of the Church in the Congo, and in other new nations. Missionaries are accepting a secondary place. The disturbing thing about this change is that the motivation seems to be political rather than Biblical. There is no fresh understanding of the doctrine of the Church, or the error of the past; the past is now repeated with a change of color.

The Church is not a missionary carrying on his program with the help of nationals. Nor is it an organization with national leadership in which a missionary is accepted as a helper.

In America or the Congo, the Church is — according to the New Testament — a body, and Christ is the Head of the body. The life that surges through the body is not Congolese life, or American life; it is the life of Christ. Each part of the body exists for the Head, and for every other part.

At a recent conference on missionary medicine, sponsored by the Christian Medical Society and Medical Assistance Program, Dr. Paul Brand — a missionary specializing in the surgical reconstruction of leprosy patients — spoke of the meaning of this relationship within the body:

"If you examine a single-celled organism such as an amoeba under a microscope, and then examine cells from the human body, you won't notice much difference. But there is actually a great deal of difference.

"The amoeba has to perform all its own functions: seeing danger, digesting food, moving away from danger.

"The cell from a human body, on the other hand, is quite specialized. There are body cells that exist only to secrete digestive juices in the dark of the stomach.

"If danger comes to a group of amoebas, or any other single-celled organisms, it's every amoeba for itself. They'll fight for available food; they'll run from danger.

"But in the human body, there are cells that give up their life if there isn't enough food for the body. When there's danger, the cells unite against it and mobilize their defenses. They don't scatter, as do amoebas.

"The church is a body."

That body exists, and is growing in the Congo. Leadership in the body should not be a matter of skin color, whether dark or light, but of recognizing the Holy Spirit's gifts.

But it is not primarily in decisions about who shall preach, or handle the money, or decide about real estate that the body proves itself. It is in the presence of danger, of persecution and death.

Fellowship deepens when pain is shared.

Six months after the Stanleyville massacre, a Congolese pastor wrote to Reverend and Mrs. Peter Stam III, former Africa Inland Mission workers in the Congo. (Mr. Stam is now home director for Canada.) After describing the ruined condition of various mission stations, the pastor concluded with these words:

"All the things of the missionaries are finished. If you receive this little letter, for I know you are thinking about us very much in your prayers, do not tie the path of our missionaries who have the desire to return to us for the work of God. To try again to build up the work of God is truly very hard, but we want the help of God and of the missionaries.

"The brethren in the land of the white man must not think that the heart of the Congolese Christian is bad toward the missionaries as some people are trying to say. All of us are praying to God and trying to call your names one by one.

"I know all the things of the missionaries are finished, there will not be much to eat any more. But if they come, we will eat our food of the Congo together. . . ."

We will eat our food together . . . both the bread of the Congo, and the Living Bread that came down from Heaven.

Here is the pattern for God's new work.

This is the Holy Communion.

Soldiers attack house suspected of sheltering Rebels. *(UPI)*

Congolese soldiers bind a captured Rebel. *(UPI)*

Handcuffed Rebel prisoners await trial for atrocities. *(UPI)*

Bibliography

The author has made use of the wealth of facts and background represented in the list which follows. This bibliography includes not only works bearing directly on the content of this book (preceded by an asterisk), but also those providing a historical and ethnographic framework for the events which have been considered.

No attempt has been made to harmonize recollections of eyewitnesses quoted in this book with other accounts. Some discrepancies may therefore be found.

ANSTEY, ROGER. *Britain and the Congo in the Nineteenth Century*. Oxford: Clarendon Press, 1962.

*CARLSON, LOIS. *Monganga Paul*. New York: Harper & Row, 1966.

CARPENTER, GEORGE WAYLAND. *Highways for God in Congo*. Leopoldville: La Librairie Evangelique au Congo, 1953.

*DOWDY, HOMER E. *Out of the Jaws of the Lion*. New York: Harper & Row, 1965.

GOLDSCHMIDT, WALTER (ed.). *The United States and Africa.* New York: Frederick A. Praeger, 1963

*HEGE, RUTH. *We Two Alone.* New York: Thomas Nelson & Sons, 1965.

HENNESSY, MAURICE N. *The Congo.* New York: Frederick A. Praeger, 1961.

JUMP, CHESTER and MARGARET. *Coming — Ready or Not.* Philadelphia: Judson, 1959.

LEGUM, COLIN. *Pan-Africanism.* New York: Frederick A. Praeger, 1962.

LESSING, PIETER. *Africa's Red Harvest.* London: Michael Joseph, 1962.

LUMUMBA, PATRICE. *Congo, My Country.* New York: Frederick A. Praeger, 1962.

MARVEL, TOM. *The New Congo.* New York: Duell, Sloan & Pearce, 1948.

MBOYA, TOM. *Freedom and After.* Boston: Little, Brown & Co., 1963.

MERRIAM, ALAN P. *Congo: Background of Conflict.* Evanston: Northwestern University Press, 1961.

*REED, DAVID. *111 Days in Stanleyville.* New York: Harper & Row, 1965.

SLADE, RUTH. *The Belgian Congo.* London: Oxford University Press, 1960.

*TRUBY, DAVID W. *Congo Saga.* London: The Unevangelized Fields Mission, 1965.

WALLBANK, T. WALTER. *Contemporary Africa.* Princeton: D. Van Nostrand, 1956.

WOLFE, ALVIN W. *In the Ngombe Tradition.* Evanston: Northwestern University Press, 1961.

YOUNG, CRAWFORD. *Politics in the Congo.* Princeton: Princeton University Press, 1965.

...oto of Dr. Paul Carlson and
...er missionaries in the Congo
...rtesy Smith, Kline & French